RECEIVING HEALING THROUGH FORGIVENESS
A GUIDE TO FREEDOM

WINSOME LEONA WILLIAMS

Scripture taken from King James Version of the Bible.

Content Editor: Suzanne Phillippa Marcellus
Copy Editor: Jo Ann Jones, Je'Ray's E-lyts Publishing
Cover Design: Teodore Thomas
Front Cover Illustration: Lindsey Steiner
Text page Illustration: Zion Tyson
Photographs: Mark Ramjohn
ISBN: 978-1-7359425-0-6

DEDICATION

This book is dedicated to my grandchildren, Genesis, Zion, Micah and Luke, as part of my legacy. I love you with all of my heart!

ACKNOWLEDGEMENTS

The manifestation of this book is proof of God's faithfulness to me.

I thank God for His Holy Spirit who leads and guides me to minister and teach on forgiveness and the wounded spirit.

To my spiritual daughter, Suzanne Phillippa Marcellus, thank you for being my encourager and fingers, putting my voice to paper.

To my grandsons Micah and Luke, thank you for assisting me with the typing and for teaching me how to use technology.

To my family and friends, biological and spiritual, thank you for your prayers and support.

CONTRIBUTORS

I am grateful to each contributor who has shared a prayer, teaching or testimony to be included in this book.

C.M.

Charlene Watson

Ethnie Ferguson

Herb and Michelle Warden

James Tyson

Joan McKoy

Dr. Judy Davis Als-Pride

Justine Clarke

Keshia M.

Kerry-Ann Connell

Nina Hart

P.M.M.E.

Pat Ramjohn

Roy Page

Sharon Scott

Suzanne Phillippa Marcellus

Yolima Quintana Estrada

PREFACE

This book is a compilation of my first book, <u>Living Free, A Guide to Forgiveness, Restitution and Restoration</u>, with additional information on the process of receiving healing of our soul wounds and the testimonies of those who have received healing through forgiving their offenders.

Know that the blood of Jesus combined with the Word of God, purges you of unforgiveness and the sins resulting from your past wounds.

"Giving thanks unto the Father, which hath made us meet to be partakers of the inheritance of the saints in light: 13 Who hath delivered us from the power of darkness, and hath translated us into the kingdom of his dear Son: 14 In whom we have redemption through his blood, even the forgiveness of sins:"
Colossians 1:12-14

It has been through difficult situations, challenges, experiences and testimonies that I have gained much of my own processing, helping me to better understand the power of God's love, grace and forgiveness.

"Before I was afflicted I went astray: but now have I kept thy word." **Psalm 119:67**

"It is good for me that I have been afflicted; that I might learn thy statutes." **Psalm 119:71**

"And we know that all things work together for good to them that love God, to them who are the called according to his purpose." Romans 8:28

"And they overcame him by the blood of the Lamb, and by the word of their testimony; and they loved not their lives unto the death."
Revelation 12:11

TABLE OF CONTENTS

CHAPTER ONE
"Understanding God's Heart Towards You"
(The Father's Heart of God)

A good father is as David describes in Psalm 68:5, *"A father of the fatherless, and a judge of the widows, is God in His holy habitation"* and in Psalms 103:13, *"Like as a father pitieth his children, so the LORD pitieth them that fear Him."* When earthly fathers taint our view of the word *father*, sometimes our view of God as a Father also is tainted. The ultimate role of a father is to have a good relationship with his children, providing love and security at all times. When we understand God's heart towards us, we will not want to continue to live a wounded and unforgiving life.

<u>GOD IS NOT...</u>

One who abandons or abuses his children.

An unjust disciplinarian even though He **DOES** discipline us in love.

Inconsistent with His love.

God loves us too much to leave us in the state we are in (wounded and unforgiving).

GOD IS...

El Elohim- God Mighty Creator

"In the beginning God created the heaven and the earth."   Genesis 1:1

"The heavens declare the glory of God; and the firmament sheweth his handywork."   Psalm 19:1

El Roi- The strong God who sees me.

"And she called the name of the LORD that spake unto her, Thou God seest me: for she said, Have I also here looked after him that seeth me?"   Genesis 16:13

El Shaddai- God Almighty

"And when Abram was ninety years old and nine, the LORD appeared to Abram, and said unto him, I am the Almighty God; walk before me, and be thou perfect."   Genesis 17:1

Jehovah Jireh- The Lord who Provides

"And they came to the place which God had told him of; and Abraham built an altar there, and laid the wood in order, and bound Isaac his son, and laid him on the altar upon the wood. 10 And Abraham stretched forth his hand, and took the knife to slay his son. 11 And the angel of the LORD called unto him out of heaven, and said, Abraham, Abraham: and he said, Here am I. 12 And he said, Lay not thine hand upon the lad, neither do thou anything unto him: for now I know that thou fearest God, seeing thou hast not withheld thy son, thine only son from me. 13 And

10

Abraham lifted up his eyes, and looked, and behold behind him a ram caught in a thicket by his horns: and Abraham went and took the ram, and offered him up for a burnt offering in the stead of his son. ¹⁴ And Abraham called the name of that place Jehovahjireh: as it is said to this day, In the mount of the LORD it shall be seen." Genesis 22:9-14

Jehovah Shammah- The Lord who is Present (with us in our pain). He allows painful circumstances to help, correct and heal us.

"It was round about eighteen thousand measures: and the name of the city from that day shall be, The LORD is there." Ezekiel 48:35

Jehovah Rohi- Our Shepherd

God allows painful circumstances to help correct and heal us.

"The LORD is my shepherd; I shall not want." Psalm 23:1

Jehovah Shalom- The Lord our Peace, Our Perfect Comforter

"And the LORD said unto him, Surely I will be with thee, and thou shalt smite the Midianites as one man. ¹⁷ And he said unto him, If now I have found grace in thy sight, then shew me a sign that thou talkest with me. ¹⁸ Depart not hence, I pray thee, until I come unto thee, and bring forth my present, and set it before thee. And he said, I will tarry until thou come again. ¹⁹ And Gideon went in, and made ready a kid, and unleavened cakes of an ephah of flour: the flesh he

put in a basket, and he put the broth in a pot, and brought it out unto him under the oak, and presented it. ²⁰ And the angel of God said unto him, Take the flesh and the unleavened cakes, and lay them upon this rock, and pour out the broth. And he did so. ²¹ Then the angel of the LORD put forth the end of the staff that was in his hand, and touched the flesh and the unleavened cakes; and there rose up fire out of the rock, and consumed the flesh and the unleavened cakes. Then the angel of the LORD departed out of his sight. ²² And when Gideon perceived that he was an angel of the LORD, Gideon said, Alas, O LORD God! for because I have seen an angel of the LORD face to face. ²³ And the LORD said unto him, Peace be unto thee; fear not: thou shalt not die. ²⁴ Then Gideon built an altar there unto the LORD, and called it Jehovahshalom: unto this day it is yet in Ophrah of the Abiezrites." Judges 6:16-24

Jehovah Nissi- The Lord our banner. His banner over us is love.

"But thanks be to God, which giveth us the victory through our Lord Jesus Christ." 1 Corinthians 15:57

"Then came Amalek, and fought with Israel in Rephidim. ⁹ And Moses said unto Joshua, Choose us out men, and go out, fight with Amalek: tomorrow I will stand on the top of the hill with the rod of God in mine hand. ¹⁰ So Joshua did as Moses had said to him, and fought with Amalek: and Moses, Aaron, and Hur went up to the top of the hill. ¹¹ And it came to pass, when Moses held up his hand, that Israel prevailed: and when he let down his hand, Amalek prevailed. ¹² But Moses hands were heavy; and they

took a stone, and put it under him, and he sat thereon; and Aaron and Hur stayed up his hands, the one on the one side, and the other on the other side; and his hands were steady until the going down of the sun. ¹³ And Joshua discomfited Amalek and his people with the edge of the sword. ¹⁴ And the LORD said unto Moses, Write this for a memorial in a book, and rehearse it in the ears of Joshua: for I will utterly put out the remembrance of Amalek from under heaven. ¹⁵ And Moses built an altar, and called the name of it Jehovahnissi:"　　　　　　　　　　　Exodus 17:8-15

Trustworthy

Jesus showed himself trustworthy, when he was on his way to heal a ruler's daughter. Though others came and delayed His journey, it did not deter Him from His original request.

"While he spake these things unto them, behold, there came a certain ruler, and worshipped him, saying, My daughter is even now dead: but come and lay thy hand upon her, and she shall live. ⁹ And Jesus arose, and followed him, and so did his disciples. ²⁰ And, behold, a woman, which was diseased with an issue of blood twelve years, came behind him, and touched the hem of his garment: ²¹ For she said within herself, If I may but touch his garment, I shall be whole. ²² But Jesus turned him about, and when he saw her, he said, Daughter, be of good comfort; thy faith hath made thee whole. And the woman was made whole from that hour. ²³ And when Jesus came into the ruler's house, and saw the minstrels and the people making a noise, ²⁴ He said unto them, give place: for the maid is not dead, but sleepeth. And they laughed

him to scorn. *25 But when the people were put forth, he went in, and took her by the hand, and the maid arose. 26 And the fame hereof went abroad into all that land. 27 And when Jesus departed thence, two blind men followed him, crying, and saying, Thou son of David, have mercy on us. 28 And when he was come into the house, the blind men came to him: and Jesus saith unto them, Believe ye that I am able to do this? They said unto him, Yea, Lord. 29 Then touched he their eyes, saying, According to your faith be it unto you. 30 And their eyes were opened; and Jesus straitly charged them, saying, See that no man know it. 31 But they, when they were departed, spread abroad his fame in all that country. 32 As they went out, behold, they brought to him a dumb man possessed with a devil. 33 And when the devil was cast out, the dumb spake: and the multitudes marvelled, saying, It was never so seen in Israel. 34 But the Pharisees said, He casteth out devils through the prince of the devils. 35 And Jesus went about all the cities and villages, teaching in their synagogues, and preaching the gospel of the kingdom, and healing every sickness and every disease among the people. 36 But when he saw the multitudes, he was moved with compassion on them, because they fainted, and were scattered abroad, as sheep having no shepherd.*"

Matthew 9:18-36

"*Trust in the LORD with all thine heart; and lean not unto thine own understanding. 6 In all thy ways acknowledge him, and he shall direct thy paths.*"

Proverbs 3:5-6

Jealous God

"For thou shalt worship no other god: for the LORD, *whose name is Jealous, is a jealous God:"*

Exodus 34:14

Omniscient - All knowing

"O lord, thou hast searched me, and known me. 2 Thou knowest my downsitting and mine uprising, thou understandest my thought afar off. 3 Thou compassest my path and my lying down, and art acquainted with all my ways. 4 For there is not a word in my tongue, but, lo, O LORD, *thou knowest it altogether. 5 Thou hast beset me behind and before, and laid thine hand upon me. 6 Such knowledge is too wonderful for me; it is high, I cannot attain unto it.*

Psalm 139:1-6

One Who Values Us- Shepherd and Overseer of our souls.

"For ye were as sheep going astray; but are now returned unto the Shepherd and Bishop of your souls."   1Peter 2:25

A Good Teacher- the Holy Spirit

"But the Comforter, which is the Holy Ghost, whom the Father will send in my name, he shall teach you all things, and bring all things to your remembrance, whatsoever I have said unto you."   John 14:26

Our Kinsman Redeemer- Jesus our Savior

"For I know that my redeemer liveth, and that he shall stand at the latter day upon the earth:"   Job 19:25

Our Salvation

"Blessed be the Lord, who daily loadeth us with benefits, even the God of our salvation. Selah."
Psalm 68:19

Jesus is your FREE PASS to Heaven.

"For God so loved the world that He gave His only begotten Son, that whosoever believes in Him will not perish, but have everlasting life".
John 3:16

If you have not yet accepted Jesus Christ as your Savior and you WANT TO BE FREE IN SPIRIT, SOUL & BODY, PRAY THIS PRAYER...

Heavenly Father, I come to you as a sinner asking you to search my heart, see the wicked ways in me and cleanse me from all of my sins. This day I surrender all my past pain and disappointment. Come in and take over my life, Jesus. Set my spirit free from sin. Set my soul (mind and emotions) free from torment of the terror by night and the arrows by day. Set my body free from all sickness and disease. I receive your complete forgiveness in my life. Thank you for your forgiveness, loving kindness and tender mercy through the shed blood of Jesus Christ, my savior.

Romans 10:9-10 says, *"If thou shalt confess with thy mouth the Lord Jesus, and shalt believe in thine heart that God hath raised him from the dead, thou shalt be saved. For with the heart man believeth unto righteousness; and with the mouth confession is made unto salvation."*

I receive your complete forgiveness in my life. Fill me with your Holy Spirit as in Acts 1:8, *"But ye shall receive power, after that the Holy Ghost is come upon you: and ye shall be witnesses unto me both in Jerusalem, and in all Judaea, and in Samaria, and unto the uttermost part of the earth."* Thank you for your forgiveness and love through the shed blood of Jesus Christ, in Jesus' name I pray, Amen.

WELCOME TO THE FAMILY OF GOD!

God promises to keep you through His grace. Jude 24-25 says, **"Now to Him who is able keep you from stumbling, And to present you faultless before the presence of His Glory with exceeding joy To God our Savior, Who alone is wise, Be Glory and majesty, Dominion and power, Both now and forever. Amen."**

"Therefore if any man be in Christ, he is a new creature: old things are passed away; behold all things are become new." **2 Corinthians 5:17**

As a young Christian I would ask the Lord, to help me not to become a stumbling block, preventing anyone from coming to know Him as Lord and Savior. As applied in Psalm 1, we are guided in this truth.

PSALM 1

Blessed is the man that walketh not in the counsel of the ungodly, nor standeth in the way of sinners, nor sitteth in the seat of the scornful.

2 But his delight is in the law of the LORD; and in his law doth he meditate day and night.

3 And he shall be like a tree planted by the rivers of water, that bringeth forth his fruit in his season; his leaf also shall not wither; and whatsoever he doeth shall prosper.

4 The ungodly are not so: but are like the chaff which the wind driveth away.

5 Therefore the ungodly shall not stand in the judgment, nor sinners in the congregation of the righteous.

6 For the LORD knoweth the way of the righteous: but the way of the ungodly shall perish.

CHAPTER TWO
"Unresolved Past Pain"

20

THE SEED OF JEALOUSY

As a nine year old child, I became jealous of my eldest sister and resentful of our mother because I thought that our mother treated her more special.

It all started out as a really happy day when my mother and father returned to Jamaica from London, England bringing home lots of goodies for the family, at least, so I thought. I suddenly noticed a large portion of the things were going in my older sister's direction. Instead of being thankful for what I received, I started to grumble, thinking that my mom loved my older sister much more than she loved me. My eyes popped open, my dream died and a heart of jealousy became alive and a new and different attitude towards my mom was birthed. Eventually my heart transformed into a sanctuary for pride.

I then started looking towards my dad as my "hero and friend", who could do nothing wrong in my eyes. I had a great relationship with my father and realized that his love was reciprocated. He had a special place in his heart for me and because of his love, I became even more prideful.

As a child, I didn't understand that the jealousy, anger, resentment and pride in my heart needed to be dealt with. Instead, like most sins, they were "swept under the rug". Growing up on the island of Jamaica, my life looked great on the outside, I had everything I needed, yet I was bitter on the inside.

In my teenage years, I realized that my dad was committing adultery. At first, I was angry but then I found reasons not to blame him for his wrong doings. Instead, my eldest sister and I pointed the blame on the ladies, thinking they were the ones throwing themselves at him.

One day I got the courage to attack one of his women at the laundry mat. I verbally abused her, then drove away, *nicely*, to my grandparents' home, where I knew I would find endorsement, protection and shelter. My grandmother wanted to rebuke me but my grandfather said, *"Adassa, leave the child alone, her mother is not bold enough to do it, so let her defend her mother."*

I wanted the woman to feel the hurt that my mother was experiencing from the affair.

HURT PEOPLE, HURT OTHERS & THEMSELVES

At the age of twenty-four, I married a man who looked just like my dad. Everyone thought I was a "whole person". I thought that my marriage would be different and better than my parents', but unknown to him, my husband could not heal the hurt of the nine-year-old girl that was imprisoned in me.

JEALOUSY MET JEALOUSY

Since the seed of jealousy towards my sister was not dealt with from childhood, it remained dormant until I became an adult and the anger surfaced. Jealousy met with more jealousy at a new and higher level and unforgiveness became alive like a monstrous tree.

The jealousy we experienced as a couple developed into mistrust. Mistrust became mental and verbal abuse which gave birth to anger and unforgiveness; this aided in the ending of our marriage. No one gets married anticipating getting a divorce. My dream of "the perfect marriage" was shattered.

During this time, my mom continued to encourage me and did her best for me, not knowing that I was still carrying my childhood hurt and resentment. Even as an adult, I would tell her, *"You love my siblings more than you love me."* Her kindness did not make a difference, because I was in my own world of selfishness and unforgiveness.

Instead of confessing my wrongs and asking the Lord and my mom for forgiveness, my next step was to prove to my mom that I knew how to bring up the perfect children. I wanted them to be kind and loving to each other and feel equally loved by me, to the point that I told my children, *"I will be content if you love each other and resent me, I could live with it."* To my regret, as life goes on, those spoken words have become my pillar of tears, but I am confident that God is a restorer of broken relationships.

In the eyes of my children, my actions towards them were perceived as more controlling than anything else. They thought I was overprotective and felt smothered by my love.

While in school, one of my daughters wrote a paper about me being her role model. Her admiration for me led me to really look at who I was and what I was modeling for my daughters. I immediately reflected on what was expected of me by God. I was aware that my anger outbursts were not a good example for them. Wanting to make sure that the world did not have another replica of my negative actions in the form of my daughters, I looked into myself to see who I really was. I asked myself, "Who has unforgiveness and jealousy in their heart?"

"Wow, I cannot seem to win." Every time I thought I was doing the right thing, it turned out to be wrong.

"For I know that in me (that is, in my flesh) dwelleth no good thing: for to will is present with me, but how to perform that which is good I find not. For the good that I would I do not: but the evil which I would not, that I do." Romans 7:18-19

My daughters experienced bursts of my anger and rage at different times because of the *unresolved past pain* in my life that needed to be addressed. Like David, I got to that place of recognizing and acknowledging my rebellion against God's Word.

What was this unresolved past pain?

Verbal Abuse!

The moment I encountered anything that looked like a shadow of my past, it stirred up anger or impatience in me. This then affected the relationship between my daughters and I, and others who I was in close contact.

Those closest to me were aware that I was not living out my fullest potential in God's love and forgiveness. I knew that I had to come to a place of total surrender to my Lord. I sought God and asked Him to show me the things He saw in me that were not pleasing to Him.

The Red Lipstick

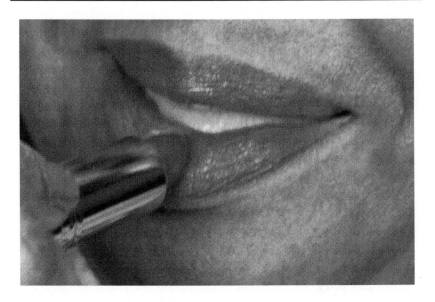

Just like David covered up his sin of adultery by committing murder (I Samuel 11 & 12), I attempted to cover my wounded heart externally with my *signature red lipstick*, looking like all was well with me.

My wakeup call came from a total stranger. I was in the supermarket minding my own business when a stranger approached me and said, "Lady, it could not be all that bad." I looked at him with fright. With defense in my voice I asked, "What are you talking about? You don't know me!" He said nothing more and departed.

It gave me food for thought. I came home, and when I looked in the mirror, the Holy Spirit reminded me of my names.

I am affectionately known as *Cheery*, which means, *in good spirits, cheerful and sunny*. My birth name is *Winsome*, which means, *attractive, appealing in appearance or character; charming (a winsome smile)*. And my middle name is *Leona, Lioness*. This name is derived from the Latin word *Leo* for lion, *meaning a person of great courage or strength*. As I stared in the mirror, I did not see any of these names reflected on my face and I knew I had to do something about it.

That night, I got my children in bed early and made an appointment with tears. I locked myself in the bathroom and cried uncontrollably.

God began to show me the areas of my life and characteristics that did not please Him and needed to be adjusted. **These traits included: anger, pride, jealousy and resentment, all of which led to unforgiveness.**

As I emptied my soul, I made a decision to release my disappointments of a broken marriage. That day, I chose to no longer allow anyone or anything to negatively influence my character. Instead, I wanted others to see the love of Christ in me. As Christians, we must be careful that when there is a problem in our lives that we don't walk around affecting the atmosphere negatively, with our faces looking like we were washed with lemon juice or vinegar.

God truly stepped in and changed my heart. This change brought about a joy in my life and I pray that you will receive this joy and be reminded that the joy of the Lord is our strength.

WHAT IS YOUR NAME?

In the Bible we learn of a man whose mother was in such great pain as she gave birth, that she named him, Jabez, meaning conceived in pain. She saw her pain as affliction, yet as Jabez grew older, he called out to the God of Israel and asked Him to bless him and enlarge his territory (1 Chronicles 4:9-10). He did not allow his name to limit his future. God granted him his request. Therefore, even if the meaning of your name is not favorable, do not allow this to taint your destiny.

Do you know the meaning of your name?

_____

What is the meaning of your name?

_____

Does it mean something positive or negative?

_____

Will you live up to the positive meaning of your name or will you rise above the negative meaning of your name?

The Confrontation

My daughters, Jeaneane and Tanique, confronted me at a time when I was asking God to search me and expose any wicked ways in my heart. God used them to let me know that I was walking around with unforgiveness towards their dad and others.

Tanique was exposed to training on Repentance, Forgiveness and Restoration, from a prior missions training. She shared her experience with me, as a gracious way of telling me that my character was not good. Initially I resented the thought of being rebuked by my daughter. Nonetheless, I went along with her, not knowing that it would be so painful to forgive and **give up my right to hurt those who hurt me**. She walked me through the process of Biblical forgiveness and restoration. God used my daughter as His vessel to teach me about His love and forgiveness towards myself and others.

Like David, I repented and asked God for His forgiveness. He forgave me and led me to ask for forgiveness from my ex-husband for all the time I was angry with him. God does not want us to live in a relationship wounded by guilt, shame, fear and unforgiveness. God wants us to walk in the forgiveness His son, Jesus, has provided.

Malachi 2:16 tells us, *"For the LORD, the God of Israel, saith that he hateth putting away: for one covereth violence with his garment, saith the LORD of hosts: therefore take heed to your spirit, that ye deal not treacherously."*

In other translations, it states that God hates divorce. So, the "putting away" is referring to divorce. It also tells us that we cover ourselves in a garment of violence. I literally was covered with that spirit of violence, anger and unforgiveness. I had RAGE.

I believe that one of the primary effects of unending strife and countless pain after a divorce or broken relationship occurs is due to the initial unwillingness to forgive. I asked my ex-husband for forgiveness for the pain from the divorce and any other pain or wounds I had caused him or our children. Meeting with him was not easy. It was very emotional for me. I asked the Lord not to allow me to cry. I was afraid my tears would be seen as weakness or cause me to step back into an angry place; with the leading of the Holy Spirit it was possible. I walked away from our meeting feeling as John 8:36 says, *"If the Son therefore shall make you free, ye shall be free indeed."*

**FORGIVENESS IS A GIFT GIVEN,
NOW A GIFT TO RECEIVE!!!!!**

In addition, I spoke with my sister about the jealousy I had towards her, which she was unaware of. This confession was shocking to my sister and it wounded her. It took time and explanation to bring restoration.

I was also led to speak with my mother. As a loving mom, she understood my emotional pain at nine years old and so, she had no difficulty forgiving me of all the hurt I had imposed on her. It was very easy to talk to my mother, because she forgave me before I even asked for forgiveness. My asking for forgiveness from family members, resulted in my mom teaching others about the importance of forgiveness. In Matthew 6:9-15, Jesus teaches us that when we forgive others, we receive God's forgiveness and if we do not forgive others of their sins, He will not forgive us of our sinful ways.

"And forgive us our debts as we forgive our debtors."
Matthew 6:12

Unforgiveness imprisons an individual.

By my own thoughts and beliefs, I had hurt myself and others. I had been in a prison of unforgiveness since nine-years-old, not knowing it.

Because of the hurt I experienced as a child, I was hurting others. **Hurt people, hurt others and themselves, and unresolved past pain can cause present pain.** Don't use your hurt to cause pain to others. Instead, **use your hurt to bring hope and healing.**

Through the leading of the Holy Spirit, I learned the importance of forgiving immediately.

- ✓ I asked God for His forgiveness.
- ✓ I forgave myself (*the nine year old imprisoned girl*).
- ✓ I went to others who had unforgiveness towards me and asked for forgiveness.
- ✓ I went to those, whom I held unforgiveness towards and released them.

2 Corinthians 1:4 says, *"Who comforteth us in all our tribulation, that we may be able to comfort them which are in any trouble, by the comfort wherewith we ourselves are comforted of God."*

Matthews 5:23-24 says, *"Therefore if you bring thy gift to the altar, and there rememberest that thy brother has ought against thee; Leave there thy gift before the altar, and go thy way; first be reconciled to thy brother, and then come and offer thy gift".*

Psalm 4:4 says, *"Stand in awe, and sin not: commune with your own heart upon your bed, and be still. Selah."*

Because God is the Lord of my life, I wanted Him to use me for His service. In order for God to use me, I needed to be a clean vessel. I had to be willing to allow God to clean my life and make me whole again through the power of the Holy Spirit. God needed to work on my un-reconciled past pains and disappointments which had manifested itself in different ways.

It was then that the spiritual surgery started. I can tell you that it was not a comfortable place in my life, but I had no choice but to surrender my will to God's will. As the Holy Spirit started His work in me, He unfolded my heart from a deep dark place of unresolved past pain.

He walked me through deliverance using Psalm 27, Psalm 51 and Psalm 91. (A sample of this can be seen on p.213). I submitted myself, by letting go and letting God do His work in me. I continue to pray for more of Him and less of me.

God knows our heart and does not want us to live a life that is wounded and filled with unforgiveness. So He will bring every secret sin into judgment or remind us of it, so that we can repent of them and begin to walk in His plan for our lives.

"For God shall bring every work into judgment, with every secret thing, whether it be good, or whether it be evil." Ecclesiastes 12:14

As I continue to walk in my God-given freedom, I thank God that He is the one who forgives all of our sins, heals all of our diseases, restores our life from the pit and crowns us with mercy and compassion. In addition, He is the one who fills our life with blessings so that our youth is renewed like the eagle (Psalms 103:3-5).

Unforgiveness will age you.
Forgiveness Renews your youth.

I have come to realize that forgiveness is not about the other person's freedom as much as it is my own freedom. The heart of God permeated my heart and transformed my unforgiving heart to one of forgiveness. I felt like my heart of stone was removed and replaced with a heart of flesh. He filled my heart with love and compassion. My heart became totally free to love even those who hurt me.

Since I no longer allow unforgiveness to stand in the way of what God wants to do in my life, In His Will Ministries of South Florida began and has grown into an inter-national outreach ministry, focused on bringing healing to hurting people globally, through our *Forgiveness Workshops*, Marriage Ministry, Hospitality, Food Outreach Programs, Health and Wellness Instructions and support to Missionaries all over the world.

In obedience to God, I ask the Lord daily, to guard my heart and give me an unoffendable heart that is quick to forgive and ready to love as Proverbs 10:12 says, "...*love covereth all sins.*"

Getting closer to God can come out of your most painful and fiery trial. So, it is important to guard your heart and reaction during your time of testing.

1 Peter 4:12-13 encourages us to live a victorious life in Christ Jesus.

"Beloved, think it not strange concerning the fiery trial which is to try you, as though some strange thing happened unto you: 13 But rejoice, inasmuch as ye are partakers of Christ's sufferings; that, when his glory

shall be revealed, ye may be glad also with exceeding joy".

1 Peter 4:7-8 instructs, *"But the end of all things is at hand: be ye therefore sober, and watch unto prayer. ⁸And above all things have fervent charity among yourselves: for charity (love) shall cover the multitude of sins,"*

I am grateful to know that the Lord has thrown our sins into the sea of forgetfulness (Micah 7:19), this brings me hope.

Romans 8:28 says, *"And we know that all things work together for good to them that love God, to them who are the called according to his purpose."*

Do you have unresolved past pain?

_____

_____

_____

What is the source of your pain?

_____

_____

_____

CHAPTER THREE
"Emotional Ways Our Soul is Wounded"

The wounded soul is a person's soul which has been hurt by a circumstance or series of circumstances that have occurred throughout the course of their life. This pain or wound has 'paralyzed' them from reaching their complete freedom in God. It is usually a dark area in the heart where the pain that was afflicted upon the individual remains hidden, yet often affects their life and relationships negatively.

There are wounds of the body and wounds of the soul. The physical wound can usually be healed with good medical care, but only God can heal the wounds of the soul. There is no medical or holistic doctor who can heal the wounds of the soul. No medical personnel can help the inner pain, wound and grief caused by a wounded soul. Jesus is the only one who can heal these wounds.

In this chapter we will focus on a few ways our souls can be wounded emotionally:

CHURCH HURT
DISSAPPOINTMENT
EMOTIONALLY BASED PROBLEMS
OFFENSE
REJECTION
SELF- AFFLICTION
SPOKEN WORDS

CHURCH HURT

"For it was not an enemy that reproached me; then I could have borne it: neither was it he that hated me that did magnify himself against me; then I would have hid myself from him: ¹³ *But it was thou, a man mine equal, my guide, and mine acquaintance.* ¹⁴ *We took sweet counsel together, and walked unto the house of God in company."*   Psalm 55:12-14

Church hurt occurs when an individual has been wounded by their spiritual leader(s) or their brother(s)/sister(s) in Christ. This can lead to anger and bitterness, causing these persons to rebel against God, stop fellowshipping with other believers or even start churches which are birth through pain.

A word spoken or action by an authority figure in the church can empower you or wound you for life. The religious traditions of men can wound you and cause you not to think about the importance of your salvation, which can eventually cause you to go astray (backslide). But God's Word reminds us that He is married to the backslider if he or she will turn from his backsliding ways.

Examples of wounds caused by Pastors:
- When a leader is found to be gossiping with other members about your spiritual condition.
- Devaluing your contribution to the ministry, whether, financial, time, or gifting.
- Unwanted sexual advancements, inappropriate relationships, harassment, molestation or rape of church members.
- Lack of empathy and compassion for your current situation.

36

☐ Intimidating you by using the Word, as a weapon of control.

☐ A leader may be insecure, jealous or threatened by your gifts and talents, as Saul was with David (1Samuel 18:5-9).

☐ _____

Examples of wounds caused by Brothers/Sisters in Christ:

☐ Competing with one another.

☐ Envy and Jealousy.

☐ Gossiping

☐ Favoritism (Partiality)

☐ _____

Here is a testimony of a woman who has experienced church hurt from both leaders and congregants, and how the Lord healed her.

***

P.M.M.E.'s Testimony

The story in John 8:1-11 really resonates with me.

"Jesus went unto the mount of Olives. ² And early in the morning he came again into the temple, and all the people came unto him; and he sat down, and taught them. ³ And the scribes and Pharisees brought unto him a woman taken in adultery; and when they had set her in the midst, ⁴ They say unto him, Master, this woman was taken in adultery, in the very act. ⁵ Now Moses in the law commanded us, that such should be stoned: but what sayest thou? ⁶ This they said, tempting him, that they might have to accuse

him. But Jesus stooped down, and with his finger wrote on the ground, as though he heard them not. [7] So when they continued asking him, he lifted up himself, and said unto them, He that is without sin among you, let him first cast a stone at her. [8] And again he stooped down, and wrote on the ground. [9] And they which heard it, being convicted by their own conscience, went out one by one, beginning at the eldest, even unto the last: and Jesus was left alone, and the woman standing in the midst. [10] When Jesus had lifted up himself, and saw none but the woman, he said unto her, Woman, where are those thine accusers? hath no man condemned thee? [11] She said, No man, Lord. And Jesus said unto her, Neither do I condemn thee: go, and sin no more."

I saw myself in this woman's place. I was having problems in my marriage and I turned to my church for help, conferring to the principles of the Bible in *Matthew 18:15-17* which says, *"Moreover if thy brother shall trespass against thee, go and tell him his fault between thee and him alone: if he shall hear thee, thou hast gained thy brother. [16] But if he will not hear thee, then take with thee one or two more, that in the mouth of two or three witnesses every word may be established. [17] And if he shall neglect to hear them, tell it unto the church: but if he neglect to hear the church, let him be unto thee as an heathen man and a publican."*

After going to the church for help in my marriage, I felt like the woman in John 8:1-11. In my marriage, I was verbally and emotionally abused. At first, we both went to a couple from a church to seek assistance, but nothing changed. I went to the leaders of the church to seek assistance from them and I felt like I did something wrong. I was told constantly what the Word of God said and what I should be doing. I felt that none of these men cared about my hurt or what I was going through at home. But, like the woman in John 8, God was there for me. God was my only hope and, "believe me," those same words that were spoken to the woman by Jesus Christ, means the same thing to me even today. These words, *"neither do I condemn you"*, meant so much to me. God wanted me to know that He was not condemning me, He was setting me free. God wanted me to be free to do His will, to do the things He purposed in my life to do.

I am electrified that God freed me from all my verbal and emotional abuse because this freedom now allows me to walk in my place of forgiveness and with an un-offendable heart, not holding grudges toward my male offenders or anyone else.

"A merry heart doeth good like a medicine; but a broken Spirit death the bones," Proverbs 17:22

***

There are times in our lives, when we seek Pastoral Counsel with the expectation of receiving empathy. Instead, we realize that our struggle, though magnified in our eyes is minimized in another's. It is important that we are aware when this occurs, so as to guard our heart from offense. Listen to how God reframed Pat's view of a disappointing meeting with her pastor.

***

Pat Ramjohn's Testimony

Years ago, while going through a rough period in my life, I decided to seek council from my pastor. To my dismay, the only advice he had for me was in the form of a scripture verse, 1 Thessalonians 5:18, which says, "In everything give thanks: For this is the will of God in Christ Jesus concerning you." At the moment I received this message I truly believed it was insensitive, terrible and simply could not apply to me because I was desperate for God to fix my situation right then. I've never lacked faith, but I have experienced moments throughout my life in which my patience has wavered. It was during my wait for an answer, that God revealed to me the lessons that I needed to learn the most. I waited years, and as time went by, I had to make the choice to hang in steadfastly until God answered my prayers because He was my only hope.

I am grateful to say that many of the struggles that kept me awake and on my knees, are now testimonies. But when I reflect back on those moments, I realize that God was teaching me through His word what long suffering actually means. God is faithful to His word and His answer to your prayer is never late. Galatians 5:22 tells us, longsuffering is a fruit of the spirit; and 2Peter 3:9 says, *"The Lord is not slack concerning his promise, as some men count slackness; but is longsuffering to us-ward, not willing that any should perish, but that all should come to repentance."*

***

As Pat applied faith, she realized that God was using Romans 8:28 to make a testimony in her life. Today she is a great example of what God's Words says in Revelation 12:11, *"And they overcame him by the blood of the Lamb, and by the word of their testimony; and they loved not their lives unto the death."*

Has your soul been wounded through church hurt, and how?

_____

DISSAPPOINTMENT

Disappointments in life can cause pain because our hope or expectation is not fulfilled. For some, the expectation of having a child and finding out they are not fertile or having a pregnancy end through miscarriage is unbearable.

Others may experience disappointment, when they set goals and find it very hard to accomplish them. This can lead to low self-esteem, depression, and unforgiveness of self. Unfulfilled self-expectation can wound one's spirit, destroy one's confidence and cause them to become insecure.

What are some disappointments you have experienced?

_____

_____

_____

My dear friend and fellow servant of the Lord, *Yolima Quintana Estrada,* gives a wonderful summary of the disappointment of Jesus' followers in Luke 24.

> In Luke 24:13-35, there is a story, which talks about two men who were completely disappointed because Jesus was killed. They were followers of Jesus and had hoped that Jesus was going to free them from the Roman government. When they saw that Jesus was dead,

they disappointedly returned to their home in Emmaus.

As they walked, a man started walking with them, whom they did not realize was Jesus, because they were too focused on the disappointment of Jesus not freeing them from the oppression of the government and shocked by His death on a cross.

When Jesus inquired about what they were talking about, they answered, "Are you the only one that doesn't know what just happened? Don't you know that they killed Jesus?" So, they began to tell him about what happened, about how Jesus performed many miracles. "We had such hope that He was going to set us free from the Roman oppression. But now that hope has died with Him."

Jesus began to show them through scripture about a Savior who had to die like this, as a sacrifice for sinners, to set people free from their sin, which was a problem far bigger than Roman oppression. He explained that Jesus died like this to give people real freedom. He said that to know God personally was true freedom and that the Savior was bringing people back to God. As Jesus spoke, they could feel something different. They began to feel the truth of His words burning their hearts. When they were near to the town that they were traveling to, they asked Jesus to stay with them awhile. Jesus agreed and when they were eating together, Jesus took the bread as He had usually done and broke it for them. As He did that, their eyes were opened to see that it was Jesus! Suddenly, Jesus disappeared from their presence, and something had changed in their lives. They had been so focused on their **disappointment** that they had missed what God was doing. Because of their wrong focus, they had given up on the teachings and promises Jesus had given them. Now after seeing the risen Jesus for themselves, everything had changed. Seeing Jesus brought revelation and understanding to their lives. They immediately ran back to Jerusalem to tell others about their new living hope. This is what everyone had been waiting for. Freedom had come!

Being caught in the pain of disappointment can block your view of God's bigger plan. As adults we must also recognize how we respond to a child's disappointments.

**Never minimize someone's hurt.
No one is too young to be wounded.**

My grandson, Micah, when he was only 7, was filled with joy and confidence as he happily showed me that his fingernail was growing. Not thinking much of it, I thought it was a hanging nail or that the cuticle needed to be removed, so I cut it off, without asking Micah if he wanted me to cut his nail.

The look in Micah's eyes told me that I had disappointed him. I immediately asked him what was wrong. He then told me, "Grandma, I am growing my nail". I then realized what I had done wrong. I was sorry for what I did and immediately asked his forgiveness. With a smile on his face he said, "I forgive you Grandma, but can you glue it back on?" I then realized the importance of that nail to Micah and not wanting to minimize Micah's hurt; I suggested that we could save the nail in a tiny cup. Micah smiled and then asked if I could put it up for him. I realized that by not minimizing Micah's hurt, it allowed him to trust me to keep his fingernail and most importantly, that he had forgiven me. Now, he also trusts me to keep his baby teeth.

EMOTIONALLY BASED PROBLEMS

Emotionally based problems are caused when we suppress our true feelings concerning a situation, they can produce physical, mental and spiritual symptoms. It has been shown that in some cases, arthritis can be acquired as a result of them.

Why does this occur?

Because God said that we cannot bear a wounded spirit. The wound can manifest itself into a physical form. Here is a testimony of a young woman whose hidden wounds affected her health, and through forgiveness the Lord brought healing.

***

"Suppressing My Wounds Revealed Unforgiveness"
Testimony by Keshia M.

On October 13, 2019 I was on a hunt to figure out what was happening with my body. I went from Emergency Room (ER) to Emergency Room and no hospital or doctor knew what was wrong with me. One ER doctor thought I was having a stroke and another ER doctor thought I was having Seizures. The things I use to do on my own I could not do anymore. I felt my entire body numb. I could not walk, I could not write and when I spoke my speech was slurred.

I was so broken and devastated by all the sudden change. I went to my Primary Care Physician and she said that I did not look well, so she referred me to a neurologist. When I entered the neurologist's office, I was surprised to see that I was the youngest patient in the waiting area. A spirit of fear gripped me instantly when I saw that. I explained my symptoms to the neurologist and he was like, "OH, maybe it is anxiety or maybe you're stressed." In my heart I knew it was NOT any of those things he mentioned. So, he suggested an MRI to see if it would help him to better diagnose my condition.

On October 25, 2019 the results came back. He told me that I had severe multiple sclerosis. My world crashed and I fell into a deep depression. All I saw was darkness ALL around me and NO light. I was desperate for more of Jesus and for his complete healing. I started on a closer walk with Jesus in my sickness. Jesus, brought me to a place of reflection and revisiting my childhood. He started to show me the times when I was wounded as a child. These past hurts were never dealt with because I never let go of the emotional abuse from my family. The physical abuse and emotional abuse from my parents, along with the spoken negative words of failure over my future. Also, a broken marriage that resulted in divorce at the tender age of twenty-three that left me gasping for air and shattered with a son.

The Holy Spirit started to show me that I never released and forgave those who hurt me deeply in my past. The Holy Spirit then told me I was nurturing unforgiveness and I needed to release it. Then the Holy Spirit began to show me why the doctors couldn't find anything in the many tests they took. As a result, the doctors felt they had to give a name to my symptoms, unknown to them it was unforgiveness. But they choose to give it a name and called it multiple sclerosis. Jesus revealed to me that the festering of my unforgiveness and wounded spirit was the leading cause to this sickness. The suppressing, harboring and nurturing of the wounds in my spirit led to this "fake forgiveness" that was crippling me internally.

Now, I'm on a journey to be made whole and free from unforgiveness daily and seeing the evidence in the improvement of my body. I am living by Romans 8:28 now and forever!

***

Do you have any emotionally based problems, if yes, what are they?

_____

_____

_____

_____

_____

_____

_____

_____

_____

_____

OFFENSE

Offense can be the gateway for anger, bitterness and unforgiveness. A word of misjudgment can leave a person in bondage. In the case of an offense, you might be judging a person who is not aware that he or she has offended you. So here you are taking on an offense that was not intended for you.

Matthew 7:2 states, *"For with what judgment ye judge, ye shall be judged: and with what measure ye mete, it shall be measured to you again."*

Matthew 18:21-22 *"Then came Peter to him, and said, Lord, how oft shall my brother sin against me, and I forgive him? till seven times? 22 Jesus saith unto him, I say not unto thee, Until seven times: but, Until seventy times seven."*

Luke 6:37-38 *"Judge not, and ye shall not be judged: condemn not, and ye shall not be condemned: forgive, and ye shall be forgiven: 38 Give, and it shall be given unto you; good measure, pressed down, and shaken together, and running over, shall men give into your bosom. For with the same measure that ye mete withal it shall be measured to you again.*

Offense is one of Satan's baits, used very often among the body of Christ. Many believers have taken on offense or put it on someone else. The choice is yours to keep carrying the weight and burden of offense. We must choose not to be offended. Psalm 119:165 says, **"Great peace have they which love thy law: and nothing shall offend them."**

As you look at the picture of this fabric, do you identify with any of these words which might have offended you?

***

C.M.'s Testimony

For a long time, I struggled with forgiving my mother-in-law. There was an issue that occurred and we had glossed over it for years without truly addressing it. I felt as though she owed me an apology, and I could not see beyond that. It was not until I attended a class on Forgiveness given by Winsome Williams that I thought about who I needed to forgive or those that I should ask for forgiveness. During that process the Holy Spirit showed me my mother-in-law at least three times and I still thought, *"She owes me an apology"*. It was at that point I was convicted by the Holy Spirit to not only apologize for my role in the breakdown of our relationship, but not to expect an apology. I wrestled with that because for years I thought I was owed an apology. Wanting to be obedient, I did what I was told by the Holy Spirit. I nervously picked up the phone and called her. As soon as she answered, we began small talk and she told me that she was in the middle of eating and would call me back. *"Yes,"* I said to myself. That was my exit, thinking I was in the clear!

Later that evening, she called me back (the moment of truth). I told her that I had attended a Forgiveness training and felt convicted to ask her for forgiveness. Initially, she was confused and did not understand what I was talking about until I mentioned the situation. To my surprise she was not even thinking about the situation and in her own words had "tucked it away a long time ago". What a relief, but just because she had tucked it away did not absolve me from needing to apologize. I took a deep breath and said, *"I apologize for the breakdown in our relationship."* My mother-in-law accepted my apology right away and told me that this was a true sign of maturity not only in the natural, but as a Christian and that I would be rewarded. My mother-in-law then said I could now pray forgive us our trespasses freely. Once she said that and accepted my apology and had forgiven me, I felt like a weight had been lifted off my shoulders and began to thank God for the gift of forgiveness and give him all the honor and glory. Matthew 6:14 says, *"For if ye forgive men their trespasses, your heavenly Father will forgive you:"*

***

Take Jesus at His word. "Father forgive them for they know not what they have done" This is His Promise to us. When you stand on the other side of forgiveness (which is forgiven) forgiveness becomes easy.

Have you been wounded by offense? If so, how?

_____

_____

_____

_____

_____

_____

REJECTION

"Thou whom I have taken from the ends of the earth, and called thee from the chief men thereof, and said unto thee, Thou art my servant; I have chosen thee, and not cast thee away. [10] Fear thou not; for I am with thee: be not dismayed; for I am thy God: I will strengthen thee; yea, I will help thee; yea, I will uphold thee with the right hand of my righteousness."

Isaiah 41:9-10

Think about the woman at the well (John 4:1-16). She came to draw water during the heat of the day, a time when no one would likely come to the well. The people of the town excluded her and caused her to isolate herself from them. Rejection can lead to exclusion which then can lead to isolation.

What did Jesus do? He gave her attention, spoke to her and didn't judge her. He accepted her with respect. He did what no one else did. He applied grace, mercy and forgiveness.

Jesus wants to do this for all of us. He does not want us to isolate ourselves with a feeling of rejection, guilt, shame, unforgiveness and disappointment in ourselves and others.

Jesus wants us to walk in freedom and victory as we overcome by the Blood of the Lamb and word of our Testimony (Revelation 12:11). After she was forgiven, she ran and told others: *"Come, see a man, which told me all things that ever I did: is not this the Christ?"* (John 4:29)

Here is a testimony of how God turned the rejection of Sharon's marriage by her mother-in-law, into a forgiving and loving relationship.

***

My Mother-In-Law and I Reconciled
Testimony by Sharon Scott

I fell in love with my beloved Greg at nine, he was ten. We attended the same church and high school while in the Bahamas. After graduation...life led us down different paths. We found each other again BUT not to the delight of his mother. This wonderful woman was a Bold God Fearing School Teacher, Women's Ministry Leader and much more.

Greg and I were married and my mother-in-law's discontentment of our union continued. I attended a Bible Study held at Cooper City Church of God, where Winsome shared from her book on Forgiveness and Reconciliation. I spoke with her after the session and she suggested I write a letter to my mother-in-law about how I felt. I was longing for her acceptance and love. I was hurting. My mother-in-law never responded to the letter.

As time passed, my mother-in-law was visiting with her sister when she suffered a near fatal heart condition. After being released from the hospital, she needed a caregiver. Much to my delight, I became her caregiver. During that time God melted her heart and love took over.

One day, we visited Winsome's home for a morning Bible study/prayer meetings. My mother-in-law loved it and still talks about it. During the meeting,

54

I reminded Winsome about her advice given years ago to write the letter. In response, as lead by the Lord, she took a long purple sash that was hanging on the cross in the room and tied it around our loins, representing us being pulled together in love. From then on we were reconciled in the love of God.... *"Therefore if any man be in Christ, he is a new creature: old things are passed away; behold, all things are become new."* (2 Corinthians 5:17) She is now my Beloved Mother and I am her Beloved Daughter.

***

Have you been wounded by rejection? If so, how?

_____

_____

_____

_____

_____

_____

_____

_____

_____

_____

SELF-AFFLICTION

Self-affliction occurs when someone causes his or herself persistent pain or distress because of the guilt they carry from the actions they have done and the words they have spoken.

It is dangerous when we choose not to repent for our sin and instead determine our own punishment. For example, Judas Iscariot betrayed Jesus for thirty pieces of silver with a kiss. After seeing what had been done to Jesus he became remorseful saying, "I have sinned in that I have betrayed innocent blood" and then went and hung himself (Matthew 27:1-7).

In Matthew 26:69-75, we witness Peter denying that he knew Christ. Peter's denial of Christ happened because his human strength was weak. He was fearful for his life as he saw what they were doing to Jesus.

When Christ rose from the dead, to show he had forgiven Peter, the angels said, *But go your way, tell his disciples **and Peter** that he goeth before you into Galilee: there shall ye see him, as he said unto you."* (Mark 16:7)

There is no sin that you can commit that God has not or will not forgive you for. Therefore, we should try as much as possible to walk in the spirit and not the flesh. 2 Corinthians 5:16 tells us, "*Wherefore henceforth know we no man after the flesh: yea, though we have known Christ after the flesh, yet now henceforth know we him no more.*"

***

ABORTION
Testimony by Kerry-Ann Connell

What can the topic of forgiveness and restoration do for someone who loves people and forgives others easily? Not much really, so I thought. It was in 2018 when Momma Cheery invited me to her seminar on forgiveness and restoration at Cooper City Church of God. Several months had passed since our initial meeting when a condensed teaching on the subject matter was presented to a transformational program group I joined the year before. Still new to Florida, having moved away from all that I knew in New York City, my mother agreed to ride with me for the hour-long drive.

We arrived early. The church was gigantic from a distance, all-consuming, until we walked in and were directed to an upper room - likened to a chamber of the heart. My eyes widened as they beheld the assortment of dainties for our consumption that day. Participants came in slowly and I searched each face for one that I might know, finally identifying a Pastor who was also in attendance. Like Momma Cheery, we met a few months earlier at a separate event while in the same transformational program. "This was interesting", I thought, "Two powerhouse women of God in one session", suddenly wondering to myself what would become of us this day.

My attempt to recall the exact details from that forgiveness session failed me, nonetheless, it was great overall. I had grown so accustomed to group sessions where I received prayer and a word from the Lord. Oftentimes, "Thus sayeth The Lord" was preceded by the plans He had to prosper me which truly gave me hope for my future. At the end of the session that day, I stood waiting for prayer. I noticed Momma Cheery a few feet away, sitting prayerfully on a stool, dressed in all white, radiating a warmth that drew me to her. Now face to face, I was asked if there was anything in my life in the area of unforgiveness that she could pray with me on - my response was no. I was almost certain that I had forgiven everyone who caused me pain whether small or large. Momma Cheery asked if she could share what the Lord is telling her, I said "Yes." She said, "Abortion!"

Her breath entered the depths of my soul and ripped a bandage from the wound that I had long forgotten, once again. It was just months prior that God revealed the same to a Brazilian Pastor, who by way of interpreter, led me through a prayer of renunciation from the spirit of Molech. The wail that ensued released tears filled with all my shame, guilt, anger, regret, self-hatred, pretense and pride. I did not realize what tremendous weight this secret sin placed on my life. The Word of God, my go-to guide for living this Christian life, tells us that our prayers will be hindered by unforgiveness – who knew that unforgiveness towards oneself was a thing?! I thought all my sins were forgiven when I accepted Christ as Lord of my life, but there are levels to the work of salvation.

Ecclesiastes 12:12 reminds us that there is no new thing under the sun. I found that the practice of abortion was the same as child sacrifice by fire to the demon Molech. (Jeremiah 32:35) Blood plasma, as we are taught in science, is the source of life. The shedding of blood, innocent or otherwise, is taken seriously by God. (Ezekiel 3:18) The Creator of all things, calls our attention to the voice that spoke to Him from the bloodshed of Abel, at the hands of his envious brother Cain. (Genesis 4:10) It was blood that secured the everlasting covenant between God and Abraham on Mount Moriah. (Genesis 22) It was blood on the door post that God honored, instructing the Death Angel to pass over His people. (Exodus 12:23) It was the blood guiltiness of David (Psalm 51:14), the man after God's own heart, that prevented him from building a temple for the God he so loved and served. Ultimately, it was the Blood of Jesus that had the power to remove every mark of reproach and charge of sin against mankind. (John 3:16)

God is a God of order. (1 Corinthians 14:40) The Court Systems of earth mirror the Courts of Heaven. (Zechariah 3:7) Like the penalty for murder being death, the same is true for the wages of sin. (Romans 6:23) The accuser of the brethren, satan, is the prosecutor that takes all sin to the courts of heaven to seek a motion for God to impose a verdict punishable by and up to death. (Revelations 12:10) The one secret I thought I could take to my grave, unbeknownst to the world, has now come to light – who could have revealed what was done in the darkness, but God? Romans 8:22 tells me that all of creation groans and Isaiah 26:21 explains, *"...the earth also shall disclose her blood, and shall no more cover her slain."*

I wondered for many years why my prayers were delayed and oftentimes denied. It frustrated me to no end that I lived on the margins of miraculous breakthrough being satisfied with what came to me by way of God's mercy and grace.

I thank God for Jesus Christ!

The Blood of Jesus promises me that if I live, move and have my being in Him then I can be free and live life more abundantly (John 10:10). We have been commissioned to spread the gospel and set the captives free (Luke 4:18). So, I share my testimony in hope that it will be the key that unlocks someone else's prison. Please believe that God reveals to heal and restore.

***

ALCOHOLISM

Alcoholism can be a wound in many families.

Who hath woe? Who hath sorrow? Who hath contentions? Who hath babbling? Who hath wounds without a cause? Who hath redness of eyes? They that tarry at the wine; they that go to seek mixed wine, look not thou upon the wine when it is red, when it giveth his color in the cup, when it moveth itself a right! At the last it biteth like a serpent, and stingeth like an adder. Thine eyes shall behold strange women and thine heart shall utter perverse things. Yea, thou shall be as he that lieth down in the midst of the sea, or as he that lieth upon the top of the mast. They have stricken me, shalt thou say, and I was not sick; they have beaten me, and I felt it not: when shall I awake? I will seek it yet again."

Proverbs 23:29-35

In some cases of alcoholism, it may be accompanied by physical, verbal and/or mental abuse. Excessive drinking of alcohol can affect relationships negatively as the person may not be in full control of their emotions and/or actions at that moment. Alcoholism can also weaken a person's ability to withstand temptation and allow them to be more susceptible to acting out differently than they normally would if they were sober.

Many families have been destroyed because of alcohol abuse. In addition, one should be careful of social drinking because it can quickly turn to abuse, especially if the alcohol abuse has been passed down through generations. Proverbs 20:1 warns, *"Wine is a mocker, strong drink is raging: and whosoever is deceived thereby is not wise."*

As you read James' testimony of how he encountered God while under the influence of alcohol and received his deliverance through the counsel of a loving youth pastor, I pray faith will arise in you to believe God for your deliverance as James did. He is now using his testimony to encourage others to know Christ as Savior.

***

James Tyson's Testimony

I've gotten into trouble because of friends doing stupid things a few times, but this time was the one that had the worst consequences. The weekend before, one of my friends, who was drunk, had given the 'bird' to someone he shouldn't have. The guy was a local thug and my friend didn't know it. I tried to stop him from doing it. The following weekend we were out again, too young to go into the pubs, but too old to stay home on a Saturday night. My two friends had been drinking and I had been doing some other stuff. As we were walking down one of the busy streets, groups of young people were milling around outside of the pubs. We didn't know it, but the same thug and a big group of his friends had seen us. As we walked on we found ourselves in an out of the way part of the town. Suddenly, the thug and two of his friends were on us. He began to severely beat my friend. I had no idea what to do and I was really scared.

Before I knew it, more of the thug's gang were surrounding me. I still don't really know what happened next, but I woke up on the floor being kicked by a number of men. I wasn't in pain though and I remember the kicks not hurting and covering up waiting for it to stop. Eventually, they left and I stood to my feet. Blood was pouring from my face and as I put my hands to my nose it felt like slush. I walked to a nearby public toilet and grabbed a bunch of paper, while sitting in a stall and walked to my church youth leader's house. I was 17 years old, had grown up in a loving Christian family and was falling away from God without knowing why. I had started drinking with my friends at 14, smoking weed and doing hallucinogenics too on a regular basis.

At my youth leader's house I remember nearly passing out and lying down on the floor. His wife was a nurse and that's why I had gone there. I loved Danny a lot. He was the best guy at my church in my opinion and an amazing youth leader. He picked me up and drove me to the hospital. I was in shock! My nose was really badly broken and the doctor thought I may have had a broken jaw. When I finally made it home in the early hours of the morning, I remember staring blankly at the ceiling as my parents looked at the damage with worried looks on their faces. I went to bed after that and there was blood on the pillow in the morning. I remembered one of the guys who had got me and ended up taking him to court. He had had a history of violence and assault, but the judges didn't send him down. He only received a fine and community service.

Something happened to me that night. Some people told me to just brush it off, but despite my best efforts, I became full of fear. I was from a small town so when I would be out with my friends now and again I would see the same group of men who had done it. The guy I took to court would hurl abuse at me and I was sure that something worse was going to happen to me. I couldn't relax and was always looking over my shoulder. My confidence was absolutely torn to pieces and I hated those guys with my whole heart.

Soon after, I started to learn kick boxing and spent a few years doing that. I grew in that area and got used to fighting on a regular basis at the kick boxing club. I became more and more used to getting hit hard and to hitting back. I decided that what had happened to me that night would never happen to me again. Years later my friend had a guy come after him at a club, I beat him down. I felt like crying. I felt like I was lost somewhere and couldn't get out.

I kept drinking and I kept doing drugs- the usual ones were later followed by different ones. It had all been fun at some point, but it wasn't fun to me anymore. I remember being at a friend's house near Liverpool at one of his amazing parties high on ecstasy surrounded by my friends and beautiful women. I heard one of them ask my friend, "Is James alright?" My friend had replied, "Yeah, he's fine. He's just really high. He's a tough nut to crack and he'll be OK." The whole night I felt like I was a shell of a person. Despite how high, I felt flat and lifeless. The come downs were even worse. I was filled up with a dark sadness and didn't know what to do.

I kept going in that life for some time until one day after a night of heavy drinking with some work friends, I bumped into an old friend from when I was a kid. Her family had moved to Israel years back to be missionaries. As we talked, she began to tell me about her life out there. She told me that her Mum had had an affair and that her family was in pieces. Then through her tears she said something so simple. She said, "But you know what, James? It's OK, because I've got Jesus and can turn to Him with this." What she said felt like a beam of light to me. I knew that that was what I needed! I remembered Jesus. That day I went to my room and on my knees repented for making such a mess out of my life and told Him how much I desperately needed Him.

About two weeks after this my life was beginning to rapidly change. I was in love with Jesus, reading the Bible loads and actually feeling God's love for me. He had begun to reveal things to me. He challenged me to go and say sorry to people that I had hurt and as nervous as I was to do it, I did it. Two weeks later I was in a pub with my friends. I was 24 and the friends that I was with were known to be hard men. They were experts in fighting and no one messed with them. I hadn't thought of the guy I took to court years back for some time. The last I heard he had gone to prison. As I sat down with my drink, I looked to the far end of the pub and there in the middle of a big group of thugs was the guy. He saw me instantly and took off his t-shirt. He was covered in tattoos. He walked over and sat opposite one of my friends who was sitting two seats away. I didn't look at him. He asked my friend, "What's your name?" They talked for a few moments then the guy stood up and sat down on the next seat over and asked the friend to my right the same thing. "What's your name?" My friend just laughed at him, "Mike who are you?" Mike was the toughest of the lot. I knew no one could touch me when I was with these guys. I knew that I knew how to fight, too, but my heart was nearly bursting out of my chest with fear. The guy stood up and sat down opposite me and said, "You look like the spit of someone who took me to court!" I looked into his eyes and said, "That's because I am that person." Every fiber of my body was ready for something to happen. There was an empty pint glass in front of me and a passing thought told me to smash it into his face, but I was so paralyzed with fear. Suddenly the guy held his hand out to me and said, "Sorry, I don't do that kind of thing anymore." A few moments passed. I held out my hand and shook his. I couldn't believe it and wasn't even sure if he meant it. He stood up and walked back to his friends. I was shaken up and went to the bar. I just stood there thinking about it all. I began to talk to God as I breathed out a big breath.

"I don't understand God why am I so afraid of that guy? I'm with my mates and no one can touch us. Why am I still so scared of that guy? It's been so long?"
God answered, "James, you are still scared of him because you haven't forgiven him."
I knew in that moment what I needed to do.
"God, I forgive him. Please help me forgive him!"
I chose this prayer. Now I can honestly say I forgive him and all the others, too. In fact, I love him and pray that he will know Jesus and be set free, too.

***

Have you wounded yourself through self-affliction?
(Abortion, Alcohol, Cutting, Suicide attempts, etc.)

_____

_____

_____

_____

_____

_____

_____

_____

_____

_____

_____

_____

_____

_____

_____

SPOKEN WORDS

Colossians 3:21 says, "Fathers, provoke not your children to anger, lest they be discouraged."

God's original design of a father is to protect his children and be the priest of his home.

The word provoke means to irritate or discourage (children) by harsh yelling or nagging and degrading their efforts. Such provocation can wound their spirit and cause them to become unforgiving, fearful, angry, timid and discouraged. This may result in a child who later becomes an adult who fails at life-efforts or has low self-esteem issues. A common quote that we have heard or said before is:

> **"Sticks and stones can break my bones, but words can't ever hurt me."**

The truth is our words can bruise, hurt, fracture and injure our spirit and someone else's. Proverbs 18:21 cautions us that, *"Death and life are in the power of the tongue: and they that love it shall eat the fruit thereof."*

As children growing up, we tend to depend on our parents to be the role models in our lives and to be the ones who bring the greatest encouragement about our potential. There have been many Godly parents who have been great examples to their children. However, in other cases, parents have misused their authority to speak poisonous words instead of life giving words into their children's future. One word spoken by an authority figure can hold you in bondage all the days of your life. These words can later become so ingrained in the child's life that they can begin to act out and live out the negative things spoken over them.

Damaging words spoken over a child can include: "You don't have any ambition; or "you are ugly, fat, and stupid." In some cases, where the parents are separated, it might be: "You act just like your daddy" in a negative way or "You have the same kind of attitude like your mom", also in a negative tone. In these cases, parents become like "false prophets" in our life, or speaking lies over us. Parents sometimes will declare that the child will never amount to anything. Even as an adult, the word can often continue to haunt the individual in marriage and other relationships as well as their careers. This can bring about great levels of insecurity and worthlessness in the person's life.

With a lack of knowledge, we might have spoken these same words or similar words to our loved ones or those who have wounded us without thinking about it; not realizing that it can affect them or ourselves negatively later in life. Remember, *"wounded people wound others"*.

For example, a parent has an unplanned pregnancy and while the child is in the womb, the words spoken over the child are: "We don't need a child now," or "We can't afford a child at this time". Since a child can hear and feel in the womb, a feeling of rejection is then planted in this child's life. Later in life these words may affect their view of God's love, thinking He doesn't accept them and cause them to doubt His destiny for their lives. Your destiny is very important, so allow God's original design to work its way in your life.

As a minister, I find that there are adults who have not recovered from negative words spoken over their lives by a parent. The pain of those words still affect them, even after a parent is deceased. I have had the opportunity to stand in the gap as the parent and repent and ask the adult child for their forgiveness for the negative words spoken because of lack of knowledge and danger of these words. Proverbs 15:4 says, *"A wholesome tongue is a tree of life: but perverseness therein is a breach in the spirit"*.

The point is, that we may be wounded by words that were spoken over us or we may have hurt others as a result of being wounded in our lives; nevertheless, never allow yourself to come in agreement with negative words spoken over your life. But if you have, there is still hope in Christ to set you free from it. The Lord was cruelly wounded by those who lied on and accused Him of things He didn't say or do.

Isaiah 53:5 depicts, *"But he was wounded for our transgressions, he was bruised for our iniquities: the chastisement of our peace was upon him; and with his stripes we are healed."*

Instead, He forgave them, because He did not want unforgiveness to hinder His children of faith, which includes you and me. Jesus is the only one who can and will help us to forgive those who have wounded our spirit through spoken words. 1 Peter 2:1 says, *"Therefore, laying aside all malice, all deceit, hypocrisy, envy, and all evil speaking"*. Wounds will heal if we allow forgiveness into our hearts and lives.

It is important that we also recognize what we have done, so that we can ask God and the person we have offended to forgive us, if and when it is possible.

Forgiveness should be a lifestyle of the believer, towards those who have offended or wounded them. Are you able to recognize when someone is wounding you out of their own woundedness? For example, because they were verbally abused growing up, they now verbally abuse you. This may provoke you to sin as they are sinning. 1Timothy 5:22 advises, *"...neither be partaker of other men's sins: keep thyself pure"*. Guard yourself from wounding others from your place of woundedness and forbid other people's wounds to wound you.

Do not allow someone else's actions, attitudes or character to determine your actions, attitude or character.

Jeremiah 29:11 says, *"For I know the thoughts that I think toward you, saith the LORD, thoughts of peace, and not of evil, to give you an expected end,"*

Psalm 139:14 says, *"I will praise thee; for I am fearfully and wonderfully made: marvelous are thy works; and that my soul knoweth right well".*

Jesus teaches in Matthew 12:35-37, *"A good man out of the good treasure of the heart bringeth forth good things: and an evil man out of the evil treasure bringeth forth evil things. But I say unto you, that every idle word that men shall speak, they shall give account thereof in the Day of Judgment. For by thy* words thou shalt be justified, and by thy words thou shalt be condemned."

Proverbs 18:20-21 says, *"A man's belly shall be satisfied with the fruit of his mouth; and with the increase of his lips shall he be filled. Death and life are in the power of the tongue: and they that love it shall eat the fruit thereof".*

James 3:1-12 says,
"My brethren, be not many masters, knowing that we shall receive the greater condemnation. 2 For in many things we offend all. If any man offend not in word, the same is a perfect man, and able also to bridle the whole body. 3 Behold, we put bits in the horses' mouths, that they may obey us; and we turn about their whole body. 4 Behold also the ships, which though they be so great, and are driven of fierce winds, yet are they turned about with a very small helm, whithersoever the governor listeth. 5 Even so the tongue is a little member, and boasteth great things. Behold, how great a matter a little fire kindleth! 6 And the tongue is a fire, a world of iniquity: so is the tongue among our members, that it defileth the whole body, and setteth on fire the course of nature; and it is set on fire of hell. 7 For every kind of beasts, and of birds, and of serpents, and of things in the sea, is tamed, and hath been tamed of mankind: 8 But the tongue can no man tame; it is an unruly evil, full of deadly poison. 9 Therewith bless we God, even the Father; and therewith curse we men, which are made after the similitude of God. 10 Out of the same mouth proceedeth blessing and cursing. My brethren, these things ought not so to be. 11 Doth a fountain send forth at the same place sweet water and bitter? 12 Can the fig tree, my brethren, bear olive berries? either a vine,

figs? so can no fountain both yield salt water and fresh."

Proverbs 16:24 says, *"Pleasant words are as a honeycomb, sweet to the soul, and health to the bones."*

Psalms 141: 3-4 says, *"Set a watch, O LORD, before my mouth; keep the door of my lips. Incline not my heart to any evil thing, to practice wicked works with men that work iniquity: and let me not eat of their dainties."*

Ephesians 5:11 says, *"And have no fellowship with the unfruitful works of darkness, but rather reprove them."*

Has anyone spoken a negative word into your life that has wounded your soul?

_____

_____

_____

Make a list of people or events that might have wounded you through words spoken.

_____

_____

_____

CHAPTER FOUR
"Physical Ways Our Soul is Wounded"

Here are a few ways our soul can be wounded physically:

ABANDONMENT
CULTURE
DEATH
DOMESTIC VIOLENCE
FALSE ACCUSATIONS
FALSE REPORTS
SEXUAL SIN

ABANDONMENT

People who suffer from a spirit of abandonment don't trust others' words or actions towards them. Feelings of abandonment can occur after the death of a loved one, especially in the case of suicide. This can also cause fear which makes them want to push others away to avoid the pain of disappointment or rejection.

In Genesis 38, we read an account of Judah's eldest son dying. As custom, Judah gave his son's wife, Tamar, to his next son, but he died as well.
Genesis 38:11 records, *"Then Judah said to Tamar his daughter-in-law, "Remain a widow in your father's house till my son Shelah is grown." For he said, "Lest he also die like his brothers." And Tamar went and dwelt in her father's house."* Years passed and Judah did not fulfill his promise, instead he abandoned her. Tamar decided that she did not want to stay in that place of abandonment, so she disguised herself as a prostitute. Not knowing who she was because of her face covering, Judah slept with her, and she became pregnant with twins. As her pregnancy became noticeable, Judah, not knowing he was the father, demanded she be burned to death. When she provided evidence that he was the father, Genesis 38:26 continues, *"So Judah acknowledged them and said, "She has been more righteous than I, because I did not give her to Shelah my son." And he never knew her again"*.

Christ experienced abandonment when his disciples fled at the time of His arrest, as well as on the cross, as He hung, he asked our Heavenly Father, *"...why hast thou forsaken me?"* (Matthew 27:46)

Have you experienced abandonment?

_____

_____

_____

_____

_____

_____

_____

_____

_____

_____

_____

_____

_____

_____

CULTURE

Many people have been wounded because of the lack of cultural awareness/sensitivity. It is important to recognize when a wound is being caused because of cultural ignorance. For example, what is respectful in one country, another may deem it disrespectful. Because of upbringing, many people are prejudice or racist, without recognizing it, believing they are more entitled than others.

For example, when people marry outside of their culture, they experience partiality in their own family, towards their partner and their children. Even at family gatherings, persons might demonstrate prejudice towards the food that was prepared by the person of another culture.

Whether it is someone's accent, fashion, food, language, music, skin complexion or anything else that differentiates us, we should not degrade another's ability, education, experience and knowledge, simply because they look or sound different than us. We should not assume that individuals with a different accent are less educated.

I have come to realize how showing kindness can make someone from a different culture than your own, feel accepted.

One day, while in the supermarket looking for a stuffed toy to give to my friend's daughter on her birthday, an attendant pulled my attention to a toy that was dressed in Christmas colors. I told her it was beautiful but that I did not want to offend my Muslim friend with the gift. To my surprise, the store attendant became excited when I said that. She explained, that as a Muslim, no one had ever said such a kind word to her or considered her feelings in that way.

I believe in loving my neighbors. I will continue to love as the Lord leads me, and invite you to do the same.

Have you been affected by cultural prejudice?

_____

_____

_____

Have you caused wounds because of your cultural prejudice?

_____

_____

_____

Paul writes in Ephesians 2:14-16, *"For He Himself is our peace, who has made both one, and has broken down the middle wall of separation, 15 having abolished in His flesh the enmity, that is, the law of commandments contained in ordinances, so as to create in Himself one new man from the two, thus making peace, 16 and that He might reconcile them both to God in one body through the cross, thereby putting to death the enmity."*

DEATH

"A merry heart maketh a cheerful countenance;
but by sorrow of heart the spirit is broken"
Proverbs 15:13

In the case of the death of a loved one or in a divorce
or separation, one can be left with feelings of
abandonment and rejection.

Jesus carried our sorrows; He was wounded for our
transgressions so that He can heal us. Jesus' spirit
was wounded but he never functioned out of the
wound. *"That it might be fulfilled which was*
spoken by Esaias the prophet, saying, Himself
took our infirmities, and bare our sicknesses."
Matthew 8:17

Jesus wants to heal every hurt and every wound, but
first we must ask Him to do so! *"Who his own self*
bare our sins in his own body on the tree, that
we, being dead to sins, should live unto
righteousness: by whose stripes ye were healed."
1 Peter 2:24

"To appoint unto them that mourn in Zion, to give unto
them beauty for ashes, the oil of joy for mourning, the
garment of praise for the spirit of heaviness; that they
might be called trees of righteousness, the planting of
the LORD, that he might be glorified."   Isaiah 61:3

I know of a young woman who was **only nine** when
she lost her mom in a tragic car accident. This
caused her to become very angry and rebellious
towards God. As she came into adulthood, she
unknowingly had suppressed this anger.

After she had the opportunity to attend one of the Forgiveness Trainings I host, God set her free from the anger and unforgiveness she had suppressed all those years. As God dealt with her wounds, she experienced His true and pure love towards her and surrendered her gifts and talents to the Lord, to be used for His glory. (John 8:36 who the Son set free is free indeed). When we allow God to cleanse our hearts and heal our wounds we are empowered to live out His plan.

After hearing this story and reading Roy's testimony of his journey of forgiving his son's murderer, I pray you will examine your heart to see if there is a wound that has been caused by expected, unexpected, peaceful or tragic death(s) of those you love.

***

"I forgave my Son's Murderer"
Testimony by Roy Page

My son Lionel Page was only 24 years old at the time of his death. He was killed on March 19, 2010 in Kansas, USA in what turned out to be a case of mistaken identity. He was shot a few times while asleep in his friend's car, waiting on a girlfriend who worked at a nightclub nearby to leave work. A guy approached the car and opened fire immediately. He later confessed in jail to another inmate that Lionel's friend was the target, and he thought the person in the car was the friend. It was only after he had done the deed, did he realized he had killed the wrong person.

I was in Jamaica when I got news of his killing and naturally I was devastated. The pain, anguish and turmoil I felt was indescribable. I cried out to GOD, "Why Him? Why me? Why was a young man in his prime with a bright future ahead of him taken so stupidly?" I couldn't understand, and the pain was overwhelming and difficult to deal with at the time. When his body was flown back to Florida and I had to go and identify him, it was the hardest thing I had ever done, but as a believer, I believed that if I laid my hands on him, GOD would raise him from the dead. I thought of JESUS raising Lazarus from the dead, and of the scripture, *"As he is, so are we in this world and greater works shall we do"*. So I believed he would come back from the dead even though he was killed for over two (2) weeks. When I failed to resurrect my son, I questioned GOD if His Words were true as in Matthew 10:8 and many other scriptures which I quoted to HIM at that time.

Since I couldn't raise my son from the dead, I had thoughts of killing the guy who took my son's life. I had thoughts of paying someone to kill him. I had thoughts of getting rid of his entire family. With all those thoughts, I also had thoughts of God's Love for me. I also had thoughts of HIS Grace and kindness shown to me. During those times and even today, I constantly speak HIS Word in my mind, quoting scriptures after scriptures, debating with God the numerous scriptures HE brings to my mind. I learned that it is HIS Word that really and truly kept me from doing something that I would have regretted and it is HIS Word that is keeping me today to live and overcome obstacles in life.

Before the funeral, I believe GOD spoke to me and told me I needed to forgive my son's killer. I again questioned GOD, "Why should I forgive him?" I was convinced he should be the one asking me for forgiveness. I was confused and unsure why GOD would allow something like that to happen to my son and then ask me to forgive his killer. For days and nights on end, I had a constant battle with GOD, but was reminded of Matthew 6:15 and many other scriptures. On the day of his burial, April 4, 2010, I yielded to the power of the Holy Spirit, and not only forgave the killer in my heart, but made a public declaration of my forgiveness at the funeral.

The bitterness, anger and frustration lingered on, however, and for the most part I just wanted to be alone, separated from people. I was still angry with GOD, but it was never to the point where I sinned against HIM. Before the trial, I believe the LORD spoke to me again and asked me to forgive his parents. So at the trial, I went over to them with tears in my eyes and told them I forgave them.

No witnesses turned up to testify as they were all threatened and fearful for their lives. Even my own family was fearful for my life. I was the only person in court representing my son, even after many warnings by family members, friends, and my son's mother, not to attend the trial. I still attended although most persons seemed to be fearful of their lives and my life because of threats issued by my son's killer and his friends, but I wasn't afraid.

Therefore, he walked from jail a free man. I couldn't understand nor accept that at the time, but the WORD of GOD was consistently saying the same things (forgive and let it go) in my heart and mind. Over the years, I constantly speak to GOD; secondly, minutely, every day and every opportunity when my mind is not engaged in something else and GOD's Word helps me to STAND even when I am not sure what to do.

I have developed throughout this great disturbance, uncertainty, and confusion in my life, a closer and deeper walk with GOD. The pain and hurt was still there after that, but it was lessened, and the burden was not that heavy. Through constant prayer over a period of time, declaring, believing and applying the Word, the burden was totally lifted. I was set free with no more bitterness and anger. I realized then that I had totally forgiven this guy for taking my son's life, and his parents for enabling and not disciplining their son who they were aware was a gunman even before he took my son's life. I realize through the Word, that people who are hurt inflict hurt on others, and forgiveness not only provides restoration for the person giving, but for the person receiving as well. I believe that GOD in his wisdom knows each person's pain and gives those persons the strength to deal with it. I no longer feel the pain, bitterness and anger although I miss my son dearly. It has not been an easy journey. There were many sleepless nights with my heart racing, belly hurting, crying, praying and wrestling with GOD. But throughout it all, I had my family, my mother, my sisters, my brothers, other relatives and friends. Special thanks to my sister and Minister, Pastor Winsome "Cheery" Williams who had my back throughout the turmoil with her unending, unceasing prayers and support. She was a major help in bringing me over this insurmountable bump in my life.

Throughout that period in my life, I learnt without a

shadow of a doubt, that regardless of how impossible and hopeless things may seem, GOD Love me, HE Loves us. GOD is able to take you out of that situation. But you must have faith and confidence in his Word. You must also be willing to forgive. Forgiveness is the fuel that drives the Christian faith and strengthens and enhances your walk with GOD. You may never overcome obstacles and situations in your life unless you are able to forgive. I thank GOD for softening my heart, cleansing my soul of the resentment and bitterness, empowering me to let go of the pain and giving me the Grace and Love to forgive.

***

Have there been any deaths in your life that have wounded your soul? (Accidents, Miscarriage, Suicide, etc.)

_____

_____

_____

_____

_____

_____

_____

DOMESTIC VIOLENCE

Domestic violence often starts with verbal abuse, when not resolved it can lead into physical abuse. Don't hesitate to seek counsel at this stage to prevent escalation.

As you read Nina Hart's testimony and charge, I pray the Lord gives you courage and clarity, in where you are at this time, in your relationship.

***

"From Victim to Victor"
Testimony by Nina Hart

My name is Nina Hart and I am here to share with you just a piece of my journey being a victim of domestic violence, but today I am a Victor, because God miraculously rescued myself and my six children from being wiped out in a staged shooting by my husband and father of our children!! We give God the glory because today we are free.

Domestic violence happens in every culture, every country, and every age, in all languages. It has no regard for religious preferences or gender. Whether you are rich, poor or middle-class, everyone can be affected. One in three women and one in four men will be a victim of domestic violence during their lifetime.

Please take heed, and let God guide, lead, talk and walk with you, and I promise that He will direct you in the way that you should go. So you can make the right choices as far as a partner and not lean to your own understanding because Proverbs 3:6 says, *"In all thy ways acknowledge him, and he shall direct thy paths."*

I did not lean on Him to direct my path, my mom knew I was going in the wrong direction but I did not listen and I paid the price but God rescued me, please don't go the wrong way. Don't do what I did. Trust God from now on so you can make a decision that will be pleasing to Him so He can spear you from the pain and anguish that comes with an abusive relationship. Trust God wholeheartedly and He will never leave or forsake you.

***

Has anyone wounded your soul through domestic violence and how?

_____

_____

_____

_____

_____

_____

_____

_____

_____

FALSE ACCUSATIONS

A false accusation is a claim or allegation of wrong doing that is untrue and/or otherwise unsupported by facts.

In Genesis 39:7-20 we read of an accusation against Joseph, the Dreamer.

Joseph was the overseer of his master, Potiphar's house, and the Lord was with him and all that he did the Lord blessed; and so his master left all that he had in his care. Joseph was handsome in body and appearance. His master's wife looked on him with lustful eyes desiring him to sleep with her; but he refused to sin against God. This made her mad so she grabbed his garment as he ran from her and called out to her servants, telling them that Joseph tried to sleep with her. She fabricated a story against Joseph. When her husband came home she falsely accused Joseph and as a result he commanded that Joseph be put into prison.

Although Joseph was in prison, God was still with him. His gift as a dreamer allowed him to be released from prison because he was able to interpret two dreams which came to pass. When Pharaoh had a dream which he could not get the interpretation, he was told about Joseph. Joseph clarified that it was not him who interprets, but God through him. As the interpretation was received, he became second in command in Egypt, letting us realize that **the false accusation could not change the original plan for Joseph's life.**

Isaiah 54:17 promises that, *"No weapon that is formed against thee shall prosper; and every tongue that shall rise against thee in judgment thou shalt condemn. This is the heritage of the servants of the LORD, and their righteousness is of me, saith the LORD."*

And Romans 8:28 declares, *"And we know that all things work together for good to them that love God, to them who are the called according to his purpose."*

Has anyone wounded your soul through false accusations and how?

_____

_____

_____

_____

_____

_____

_____

_____

_____

FALSE REPORTS

False reports from a doctor can also wound your spirit. My mother was only 46 years old when she realized that her body was making some changes in her health. At first she thought it was a pinched nerve. The general practitioner did not see anything unusual, but referred her to a neurologist because of the numbness she was experiencing in her right hand. During our visit to the neurologist, without any tests being done and no compassion in his voice he spoke these words, "We can't do anything for you because it is multiple sclerosis". This is a disease in which the immune system attacks the protective covering of the nerve endings.

My mom got the shock of her life with this diagnosis because at the time there was no cure and very little treatment available to her on the Island. As this report was not what my mother was expecting, her body becoming fearful as these *words* of hopelessness and death was spoken in her hearing.

Proverbs 18:21 tells us that, **"Death and life are in the power of the tongue: and they that love it shall eat the fruit thereof."** These words began to come to pass in my mother's life as the same sensation of numbness in her right hand was also in her legs.

As a family we did not believe the false report of the doctor, she was only 46 years old and in the prime of her life. She made several trips to other doctors locally and overseas. As the doctor's studied her family history, they discover that it was early menopause symptoms and not multiple sclerosis.

Though the initial false report of the doctor's diagnosis started to cripple my mom's dreams, the joy of the Lord became her strength. Faith arose when she started having grandchildren. She started to hope again and began on a new page in life; investing quality time with her family and this new place of being a grandmother. She was an amazing woman who lived beyond the doctor's false report.

***

Doctor False Report Testimony
By Ethnie Ferguson

After the pediatrician examined my 9 year old daughter, he recommended further tests to be done. Upon returning to him with the report, he informed me that she had bronchitis and proceeded to write a prescription for medication to treat it. I took the prescription and proceeded to the pharmacy, but somehow felt that the Lord wanted me to seek a second opinion before I filled it. I then scheduled an appointment with another pediatrician who reviewed the lab report. I shared with her the diagnosis given by the prior doctor and she informed me that my daughter did not have bronchitis, instead it was a bit of heart burn.

Had I administered the prescribed medicine to my daughter, it probably would have had a negative side effect on her body. My daughter is now a thriving and successful 24-year old who has never suffered from bronchitis. I praise the Lord for speaking to my heart to seek a second opinion.

***

Have you been wounded by false reports? If so, how?

_____

_____

_____

_____

_____

_____

_____

_____

_____

_____

_____

_____

_____

_____

SEXUAL SIN

Sexual sins that we commit or are committed against us, such as adultery, bestiality, fornication, homosexuality, lust, molestation, pedophilia, rape and more, wound our souls.

If you have endured sexual abuse of any kind, it is important that you recognize it was not your fault. As we read 2 Samuel 13:7-34, of how Tamar was raped by her brother. This rape gave birth to secondhand unforgiveness in her brother, Absalom, who came to her defense.

7 Then David sent home to Tamar, saying, Go now to thy brother Amnon's house, and dress him meat. 8 So Tamar went to her brother Amnon's house; and he was laid down. And she took flour, and kneaded it, and made cakes in his sight, and did bake the cakes. 9 And she took a pan, and poured them out before him; but he refused to eat. And Amnon said, Have out all men from me. And they went out every man from him. 10 And Amnon said unto Tamar, Bring the meat into the chamber, that I may eat of thine hand. And Tamar took the cakes which she had made, and brought them into the chamber to Amnon her brother.

11 And when she had brought them unto him to eat, he took hold of her, and said unto her, Come lie with me, my sister. 12 And she answered him, Nay, my brother, <u>do not force me</u>; for no such thing ought to be done in Israel: do not thou this folly. *13 And I, whither shall I cause my shame to go? and as for thee, thou shalt be as one of the fools in Israel. Now therefore, I pray thee, speak unto the king; for he will not withhold me from thee.*

14 Howbeit he would not hearken unto her voice: but, being stronger than she, forced her, and lay with her. 15 Then Amnon hated her exceedingly; so that the hatred wherewith he hated her was greater than the love wherewith he had loved her. And Amnon said unto her, Arise, be gone. 16 And she said unto him, There is no cause: this evil in sending me away is greater than the other that thou didst unto me. But he would not hearken unto her. 17 Then he called his servant that ministered unto him, and said, Put now this woman out from me, and bolt the door after her. 18 And she had a garment of divers colours upon her: for with such robes were the king's daughters that were virgins apparelled. Then his servant brought her out, and bolted the door after her. 19 And Tamar put ashes on her head, and rent her garment of divers colours that was on her, and laid her hand on her head, and went on crying. 20 And Absalom her brother said unto her, Hath Amnon thy brother been with thee? but hold now thy peace, my sister: he is thy brother; regard not this thing. So Tamar remained desolate in her brother Absalom's house.

21 But when king David heard of all these things, he was very wroth. **22 And Absalom spake unto his brother Amnon neither good nor bad: for Absalom _hated_ Amnon, because he had forced his sister Tamar.** 23 And it came to pass after two full years, that Absalom had sheepshearers in Baalhazor, which is beside Ephraim: and Absalom invited all the king's sons. 24 And Absalom came to the king, and said, Behold now, thy servant hath sheepshearers; let the king, I beseech thee, and his servants go with thy servant. 25 And the king said to Absalom, Nay, my son, let us not all now go, lest we

be chargeable unto thee. And he pressed him: howbeit he would not go, but blessed him. ²⁶ Then said Absalom, If not, I pray thee, let my brother Amnon go with us. And the king said unto him, Why should he go with thee?

²⁷ But Absalom pressed him, that he let Amnon and all the king's sons go with him. ²⁸ **Now Absalom had commanded his servants, saying, Mark ye now when Amnon's heart is merry with wine, and when I say unto you, Smite Amnon; then kill him, fear not: have not I commanded you? be courageous, and be valiant. ²⁹ And the servants of Absalom did unto Amnon as Absalom had commanded.** Then all the king's sons arose, and every man gat him up upon his mule, and fled. ³⁰ And it came to pass, while they were in the way, that tidings came to David, saying, Absalom hath slain all the king's sons, and there is not one of them left. ³¹ Then the king arose, and tare his garments, and lay on the earth; and all his servants stood by with their clothes rent. ³² And Jonadab, the son of Shimeah David's brother, answered and said, Let not my lord suppose that they have slain all the young men the king's sons; for Amnon only is dead: **for by the appointment of Absalom this hath been determined from the day that he forced his sister Tamar.** ³³ Now therefore let not my lord the king take the thing to his heart, to think that all the king's sons are dead: for Amnon only is dead. ³⁴ But Absalom fled. And the young man that kept the watch lifted up his eyes, and looked, and, behold, there came much people by the way of the hill side behind him.

Absalom held on to the sin of secondhand unforgiveness for over two years and plotted against his brother Amnon. We will discuss **Secondhand Unforgiveness in Chapter 6.**

Amnon never asked for forgiveness from his sister, after he raped her. His behavior was not one of repentance and because of his action, he was killed by Absalom (his brother) for the crime he committed.

Now we will read Joan's testimony of how the Lord helped her to forgive her sexual offender, after holding on to bitterness, hurt, pain, shame and unforgiveness for 36 years.

***

"I Was Only Nine..."
Testimony by Joan McKoy

My name is Joan McKoy. I was only nine years old when my world fell apart. The unthinkable took place in my life when a friend of my sister made several detours on any given Saturday before taking me to my sister's home, as he was asked to do. Instead, he took me to his house where he sexually molested me. I was ashamed and frightened because I grew up in a home where my mom was physically and mentally abused by my dad. I was afraid to disclose what was happening to me, because whenever anything bad happened to my siblings or me, our dad always blamed our mother. Wanting to protect my mother, I did not say a word fearing that she would be physically beaten and mentally chastised by my dad.

After many years went by, I sat with my mom and shared with her all that had happened to me. For all those years, I blamed my sister who was acquainted with this man. I blamed her for bringing him in our home that allowed him to violate my life the way he did. My sister did not know I was angry at her and that I had unforgiveness in my heart towards her. To sum it up in the right words, I was bitter for all those years.

Not knowing the damage that life would have caused, at the age of 45, I was diagnosed with breast cancer. So a friend invited me for a walk in the park. God had used her in my life at different times for many years. Wow! That was the day that Jesus unveiled my shame, hurt, unforgiveness and all the bitterness that I had in my heart. But, because of the love and mercy of Father God, I have been truly healed, delivered and set free.

From the day I was confronted and taken into the park until today, I've been a free woman telling everyone and anyone that comes into my path that Jesus Christ is the one they should desire and He can and will set them free. 2 Corinthians 4:7 became so real to me, it says God has Treasures in Earthen vessels. I am one of those Earthen vessels that God has placed his Treasure of love and forgiveness. In my heart, I know my life will never be the same. Romans 8:1 reminds me, *"There is therefore now no condemnation to them which are in Christ Jesus, who walk not after the flesh, but after the Spirit."* I've been set free by the love of God and by the Holy Spirit that lives and dwells in my soul. We serve the only wise God who is able to keep us from falling into sin.

***

Have you been wounded through forced prostitution, molestation, rape or any other sexual crime committed against you?

_____

_____

_____

_____

_____

For some, these violations against them, have opened doors to a variety of sexual sins. God desires to heal your brokenness and deliver you from every path the sins committed against you have led you down.

Sexual involvements outside of the marriage, whether in adultery or fornication has an effect on us. Apostle Paul admonishes in 1 Corinthians 6:18 to, *"Flee fornication. Every sin that a man doeth is without the body; but he that committeth fornication sinneth against his own body."*

Sexual activity during a dating relationship or engagement can invite a wounded soul into a future marriage. When the novelty of the 'secret lustful relationship' has ended and commitment and responsibility become a reality within the bonds of marriage, often the novelty of 'stealing love' ends. One party's sexual expectation may no longer seem as if it is being met and they may even seek another avenue to selfishly fulfill this unrealistic desire. This selfish mindset can then wound the marriage. *"But whoso committed adultery with a woman lacketh understanding; he that doeth it destroyeth his own soul" (Proverbs 6:32).*

As we study 1 Corinthians 6:9, 13-17, 19-20, we see more clearly the weight that comes with sexual sin. As believers, our bodies belong to the Lord, and should not be joined to anyone outside of our spouses.

"9 Know ye not that the unrighteous shall not inherit the kingdom of God? Be not deceived: neither fornicators, nor idolaters, nor adulterers, nor effeminate, nor abusers of themselves with mankind...13 Meats for the belly, and the belly for meats: but God shall destroy both it and them. Now the body is not for fornication, but for the Lord; and the Lord for the body. 14 And God hath both raised up the Lord, and will also raise up us by his own power. 15 Know ye not that your bodies are the members of Christ? shall I then take the members of Christ, and make them the members of an harlot? God forbid. 16 What? know ye not that he which is joined to an harlot is one body? for two, saith he, shall be one flesh. 17 But he that is joined unto the Lord is one spirit. 19 What? know ye not that your body is the temple of the Holy Ghost which is in you, which ye have of God, and ye are not your own? 20 For ye are bought with a price: therefore glorify God in your body, and in your spirit, which are God's."

If you have found yourself struggling with this sin, be willing to be open to the Lord about it as He is already aware of our "hidden sin".

As God gives you specific conviction on any sexual related issues that we have discussed as well as masturbation or watching porn, you must be willing to deal with them immediately so that its power may be broken. Confession of sin needs to be specific for the purpose of deliverance. *"For God shall bring every work into judgment, with every secret thing, whether it be good, or whether it be evil". Ecclesiastes 12:14*

Have you been wounded through any sexual acts/relationships?

_____

_____

_____

_____

_____

_____

_____

_____

_____

_____

_____

_____

CHAPTER FIVE
"Spiritual Ways Our Soul is Wounded"

Many who have been wounded become angry, unforgiving, resentful, fearful and bitter. The fruit of these wounds often affect our lives and the lives of others. When wounds are not taken care of, they can take root in the lives of our descendants, thus creating a generational pattern of anger, bitterness, fear and unforgiveness. Ezekiel 18:2 makes reference to the proverbs that states, "... *the fathers have eaten sour grapes, and the children's teeth are set on edge"*.

These curses can be passed down from father to son and generations thereafter.

Example: Mary's grandmother had unforgiveness towards her sister for a number of years and so because of Mary's love for her grandmother she felt that it was her right to also demonstrate unforgiveness towards her grandaunt.

The Bible also speaks of a "wounded spirit" in Proverbs 18:14, *"The spirit of a man will sustain his infirmity but a wounded spirit who can bear?"* Since, we cannot bear a wounded and broken spirit, we should not attempt to carry this burden. If you are broken, crippled and walking wounded, then you are not whole. The wound can manifest through your emotions, anger, bitterness, bad attitude and sometimes in the case of sickness and many other forms.

Two of the ways we can be wounded spiritually are by **FALSE PROPHETS** and the **ORPHAN SPIRIT**.

FALSE PROPHETS

"The prophets prophesy falsely, and the priests bear rule by their means; and my people love to have it so: and what will ye do in the end thereof?" -Jeremiah 5:31

When those who claim to be prophets of God, speak a word over one's life that brings condemnation, stagnation and cannot be backed in scripture, this can cause a long term wound in one's life.

These same men/women may also bring a "word" of prosperity that is linked to a financial sacrificial seed. Many are also wounded from prophecies that tickle their ears, Apostle Paul warns in 2 Timothy 4:3-4, *"For the time will come when they will not endure sound doctrine, but according to their own desires, because they have itching ears, they will heap up for themselves teachers; 4 and they will turn their ears away from the truth, and be turned aside to fables."*

Have you been wounded by false prophecies?

_____

_____

_____

_____

_____

_____

ORPHAN SPIRIT

My dad, Winston, while growing up, had no idea that he was an orphan until a neighbor brought it to his attention. She asked him the question, "Have you ever thought about why your skin is not as black as the rest of the Mitchell's family?" He answered, "No". But that question opened a large can of worms with many questions and answers at the same time. My father's skin tone was a couple shades lighter than his family and his hair texture was soft and curly, unlike his siblings.

He thought to himself, "Now it's making more sense why my sister always gets me in trouble. Like when she stole a piece of potato pudding, then cast the blame on me and it was hard to prove my innocence."

My father spent many nights and days outdoors under a pimento tree by himself dreaming that one day he would build a large home on a hill like Mr. Merison, a man he admired. This became his greatest encouragement to live.

As years passed by, he felt the need to learn carpentry like Mr. Merison, but the Mitchel family would not support him in this trade. They didn't see this as a career choice for the educated. This denial gave him the courage to ask the question that had haunted his mind for many years.

He asked his older sister, "Am I adopted?" She responded, "Who told you that?" He replied, "All I need to know is, is this true?" The place was silent for a moment with no answer, then she commented, "All you need to know is that you belong in this family." This response pushed my father to gather all of his belongings and in time he made his way to Kingston, Jamaica.

The Bus reached its final destination, he got off not knowing where he was going to spend the night. He shared his story with the guard, who was compassionate and allowed him to sleep in one of the buses. The next day he met Archer, who became his lifelong friend and helped him to get a job learning to build bus frames. It was not long before the owner of the bus business offered him a night job at their club. Time passed, he became a carpenter, worked two jobs and met the girl, my mom, who he wanted to marry. He wasted no time and asked, "If I'm a carpenter and you're a lady, will you marry me?" She laughed at him and said, "You need to talk to my father." After her dad lectured him, he gave him permission to marry her.

Later on, by divine intervention, Archie introduced my dad to his eldest biological sister, who carried his birth name Mullings. Through this encounter, he learned of his family. Although he decided to set aside the name Mitchell and carry the name Mullings, he never got over the fact that he was an orphan. He had an opportunity to meet his other siblings, but his parents had already died. Thankfully, his relationship to his adoptive family was restored.

My dad came to realize that material things could not remove this orphan spirit. As children, he shared his story with anyone who would listen- even my siblings and I. Before he died, I had the opportunity to speak with him, lead him to Christ and encourage

103

him to let go of that orphan spirit and I believe he did.

"According as he hath chosen us in him before the foundation of the world, that we should be holy and without blame before him in love: Having predestinated us unto the adoption of children by Jesus Christ to himself, according to the good pleasure of his will," Ephesians 1:4-5

***

Recognizing the Orphan Spirit
By Dr. Judy Davis Als-Pride

Not so long ago, I heard someone ask what is an orphan spirit? No one in the group really had a satisfying answer. Something in my core began to resonate in me, there was a familiarity with the term and I went home and began to research the orphan spirit. Author of "Is the Orphan Spirit Operating in in My Life", Curt Landry's definition gave me revelation and further acknowledgement to the goodness of God in my life. Eureka! The definition fit me to a tee. It defined me and fit like a glove. That is, until I accepted Jesus into my life and let go of past abuse and let go of past transgressions.

I grew up in a very abusive household, devoid of God for the most part. My step-father abused my mom to the point she could no longer mentally or physically survive in the environment. This motivated her to leave him and, unfortunately, her children as well. I, being the eldest became, the substitute for her. I was abused physically, sexually and emotionally. I was belittled and ridiculed to break my young, innocent spirit. Consequently, I became filled with guilt, shame and was filled with feelings of unworthiness. I believe very often what we think, our very thoughts, convinces our heart and yes, even our body to believe we are "less than." It puts us in the realm of dis-ease, loneliness and abandonment. I felt discarded by my mom and betrayed by my stepfather. Certainly I was orphaned, but I didn't realize I was being overtaken by an orphan spirit. I named my feelings guilt, shamefulness, not worthy to be loved by God or by humans. I named it alienation. I did most things alone and excelled at most things I was charged to do. I felt I didn't need anybody. I was repelled by human touch for fear they would hurt me, or worst, break the protective shell I had allowed around me. I felt I was unforgiveable and full of the burden of unforgiveness.

BUT GOD!

God's Word in Psalm 10:14 declares, *"Thou hast seen it; for thou beholdest mischief and spite, to requite it with thy hand: the poor committeth himself unto thee; thou art the helper of the fatherless."*

When I finally stopped running from God, submitted my life, confessed my sins and opened my heart to Jesus and the Holy Spirit, I had a sensation of coming out of a vacuum, of shedding a feeling of oppression. It was a metamorphosis; a stepping out of what I now know was an orphan spirit into the Spirit of Adoption as a daughter of the Most High God. I was "Born Again!" It was a second birth. I was able to come to God as a child, accepting my Abba Father, my Daddy's infinite love.

I learned through the Word of God that, *"Therefore if any man be in Christ, he is a new creature: old things are passed away; behold, all things are become new."*
2 Corinthians 5:17

Romans 8:15 decrees: *"For ye have not received the spirit of bondage again to fear; but ye have received the Spirit of adoption, whereby we cry, Abba, Father."*

Jesus said in John 14:18, *"I will not leave you comfortless; I will come to you."*

When I became "Born Again", an exchange took place. That negative, oppressive unforgiving spirit that I now can name "Orphan spirit" was replaced by the Holy Spirit of unconditional love, grace, mercy and yes forgiveness. It was a process. The more my prayer life and relationship with the Lord increased, the more I was able to forgive myself and accept the unconditional love of God. I was able to enter into healthy relationships. I was able to love and hug without feeling vulnerable. God heard my cry, GOD helped me. God healed and renewed my mind, healed and renewed my heart, healed and renewed my spirit. I can declare in the name of Jesus, I am loosed and I am healed. I am made in the image of God, wonderfully and marvelously made. I am a woman of value, I am a woman of worth, I am a woman loved by God saved and forgiven.

Although it took some time, I did come to a season of spiritual growth to forgive my mother and I was able to forgive my step-father and lead him to Jesus. Hallelujah! Today I walk in the spirit of freedom because to be free in Jesus is to be free indeed!

***

Have you been oppressed by an orphan spirit?

_____

_____

_____

_____

> ***Don't allow your wounds to color the pages of your life and then mistreat others the way you were mistreated. You might be preventing someone from fulfilling the call of God on their life.***

Ask God if there are any other ways that your soul has been wounded. He knows and sees them before you ask.

_____

_____

_____

_____

_____

In the coming chapters we will learn how to receive healing for our wounded soul as we walk through the process of forgiveness.

CHAPTER SIX
"The Poison of Unforgiveness"

"Let all bitterness, and wrath, and anger, and clamor, and evil speaking, be put away from you, with all malice" Ephesians 4:31

A word spoken in anger can taste like a bitter cup to the offender. Unforgiveness is likened to someone drinking deadly poison and expects that the person they chose not to forgive will die, while they remain in a state of unforgiveness.

UNFORGIVENESS

Unforgiveness corrodes and destroys faith.

Unforgiveness cripples love.

Unforgiveness destroys confidence.

Unforgiveness delays restoration.

Unforgiveness eats away peace.

Unforgiveness encourages bad memories.

Unforgiveness invades and silences the soul.

Unforgiveness is a wall between you and God.

Unforgiveness keeps records of wrong.

Unforgiveness kills fellowship.

Unforgiveness quenches the Holy Spirit.

Unforgiveness reduces hope of eternal life.

Unforgiveness shatters hope.

Unforgiveness stops the courage to love again.

UNFORGIVENESS	FORGIVENESS
Looks back.	Looks ahead.
Chooses judgment.	Chooses mercy.
Says, "Judgment is mine".	Says, "Judgment is the Lord's"
Holds on to their rights.	Gives up their rights to God.
Holds the person accountable for the wrong that was done to them.	Releases the person from the wrong that was done to them.
Causes self-imprisonment.	Sets you free.
Can cause slow death.	Causes you to live.
Causes you to relive the past.	Allows you to live in the present.
Has no feeling of regret and does not admit to any wrong deed.	Repents of wrong doing and feeling of regrets.
Holds on to what they feel belongs to them.	Brings about restitution.
Is overcome by evil.	Overcome evil with goodness.
Encourages the flesh to remain in bondage.	Crucifies the flesh.

"Be not overcome of evil, but overcome evil with good".
Romans 12:21

"The discretion of a man deferreth his anger, and it is his glory to pass over a transgression"
Proverbs 19:11

"If we confess our sins, he is faithful and just to forgive us our sins, and to cleanse us from all unrighteousness". 1 John 1:9

"Wrath is cruel, and anger is outrageous; but who is able to stand before envy?" Proverbs 27:4

"Cast out the scorner, and contention shall go out, yea, strife and reproach shall cease" Proverbs 22:10

"And if children, then heirs; heirs of God and joint heirs with Christ, if so be that we suffer with Him, that we may be also glorified together" Romans 8:17

"For I reckon that the sufferings of this present time are not worthy to be compared with the glory which shall be revealed in us" Romans 8:18

The Parable of the Unforgiving Servant
Matthew 18:21-35

21 Then came Peter to him, and said, Lord, how oft shall my brother sin against me, and I forgive him? till seven times? 22 Jesus saith unto him, I say not unto thee, Until seven times: but, Until seventy times seven. 23 Therefore is the kingdom of heaven likened unto a certain king, which would take account of his servants. 24 And when he had begun to reckon, one was brought unto him, which owed him ten thousand talents. 25 But forasmuch as he had not to pay, his lord commanded him to be sold, and his wife, and children, and all that he had, and payment to be made. 26 The servant therefore fell down, and worshipped him, saying, Lord, have patience with me, and I will pay thee all. 27 Then the lord of that servant was moved with compassion, and loosed him, and forgave him the debt. ²⁸ *But the same servant went out, and found one of his fellowservants, which owed him an hundred pence: and he laid hands on him, and took him by the throat, saying, Pay me that thou owest.* ²⁹ *And his fellowservant fell down at his feet, and besought him, saying, Have patience with me, and I will pay thee all.* ³⁰ *And he would not: but went and cast him into prison, till he should pay the debt.* ³¹ *So when his fellowservants saw what was done, they were very sorry, and came and told unto their lord all that was done.* ³² *Then his lord, after that he had called him, said unto him, O thou wicked servant, I forgave thee all that debt, because thou desiredst me:* ³³ *Shouldest not thou also have had compassion on thy fellowservant, even as I had pity on thee?* ³⁴ *And his lord was wroth, and delivered him to the tormentors, till he should pay all that was due unto him.* ³⁵ *So likewise shall my heavenly Father do also unto you, if ye from your hearts forgive not every one his brother their trespasses.*

This story teaches us that forgiveness is very important because it can also affect our eternal destination. Unforgiveness opens the door that allows the tormentor (Satan) to have control in our lives and robs us of the blessings that God has in store for us.

WHAT'S AT THE ROOT?

The root of a tree is what absorbs nutrients from the soil and in return causes the plant to become healthy and look good. Without the roots, the plant would collapse and die.

Maybe you can identify with the process plants go through, because you have been walking around looking good on the outside, but under the surface, is a root of bitterness and anger eating away your joy, peace and love, and feeding on the bitterness that is fertilizing a foundation of hatred.

"Looking diligently lest any man fail of the grace of God; lest any root of bitterness springing up trouble you, and thereby many be defiled"   Hebrews 12:15

As a child, I ate a lot of fruits, during the summer. The richness in certain fruits would cause my body to form boils and cysts. I remember how painful the boils were but I would not tell my mother or grandmother about it until the pain became unbearable causing me to limp. To get to the root of the boils, they created a home remedy which consisted of spicy hot pepper leaves and warm olive, castor or coconut oil. It was then placed on top of the boil repeatedly for several days. During the process, pressure was applied to the area which worsened the pain. In the midst of my pain, there was a certain amount of love I would hear from my grandmother and mother. Some of the words coming from my grandmother would be, "We must get to the root of the boil in order to destroy it". Can you imagine love in this process!!?

At first I did not see it as love, all I saw was the pain. This pain is likened to the pain of forgiveness. It is painful to give up your right to hurt someone that has hurt you. Yet, as you release your life from unforgiveness you will walk into your blessing. God has great plans for your life, so remember...

"Hurt people, hurt others.
Healed people heal others with
love and forgiveness."

"Stand fast therefore in the liberty wherewith Christ hath made us free, and be not entangled again with the yoke of bondage."   Galatians 5:1

We cannot be in a right relationship with Christ Jesus, if we have unforgiveness in our hearts. For healing to take place, there must come a time when we get to the root of our unforgiveness, bitterness and rage.

During the forgiveness classes I conduct, one of the demonstrations that I use to illustrate what unhealed wounds look like is using a band-aid that is so close in color to my flesh that it is often difficult for the participants to distinguish the band-aid from my skin. (I place the band-aid on my skin and proceed with the class). People often place band-aids over their wounds and like my demonstration, the band-aids blend so well that we forget they're there.

We go about our day to day lives forgetting about the band-aids that we have placed on our wounds. It isn't until someone says or does something that reminds us of the said hurt and unforgiveness that we remember what is under the band-aid that blended so well with our skin.

The existence of the wound is displayed by how we respond to that particular person/ situation during the time of offense and it is at that time we realize we must now remove the band-aid. In other words, we need to now go back to the wound, open it up and clean it up. It is then and only then (once the wound has been exposed and cleaned up) that we are in a position to not only heal, but to also forgive.

I will also liken unforgiveness to a medical doctor who is expected to use a lancet to cut open the top of an infected area and apply pressure around the inflamed area to force out the core or root of the infection. **It is extremely painful!** So, we avoid exposing the problem to the doctor for fear of the pain to remove the cysts. I know there is modern medicine with lasers that can cut thorough any cysts

or tumor, but **ONLY Jesus' forgiveness will cut through our woundedness and bring about true healing in our lives.**
What is it in our life of unforgiveness that we would rather endure the throbbing pain, headaches, sickness, anger, bitterness, fear, doubt, that Our Great Physician, God our father wants to free us from? Why not allow Him to cut through the core or root of unforgiveness and set you free to live again?

In His freedom, we are free indeed!

Don't allow the infection of unforgiveness to make you sick emotionally, mentally, physically and spiritually anymore. The sins of bitterness, unforgiveness, resentment, anger and rage are all poison in your bloodstream and can hinder your spiritual growth. Jesus paid it all for our sins through His blood.

Unforgiveness will hinder the flow of God's Spirit in your life. In addition, unforgiveness allows your offender to live rent/mortgage free in your body, heart and mind, as you are constantly thinking about the offense and seeing yourself as a victim instead of victorious in Christ Jesus.

God has given us the tools to pluck up and destroy any root that is not healthy in our lives and all we need to do is expose it and give it to Him, because He knows how to fix it.

"And have no fellowship with the unfruitful works of darkness, but rather reprove them. 12 For it is a shame even to speak of those things which are done of them in secret. 13 But all things that are reproved are made

116

manifest by the light: for whatsoever doth make manifest is light."   Ephesians 5:11-13

Sad to say, but many are still bearing grudges or malice towards dead relatives and friends. As it is said, there is no repentance in the grave.

Psalm 103 teaches that the Lord forgave **NOT SOME, BUT All** our iniquities, healed **ALL** our diseases, redeemed our lives from destruction and crowned us with lovingkindness and tender mercies. *He satisfies our mouth with good things so that our youth is renewed like the eagles.*

UNFORGIVENESS CAUSES DECAY

Unforgiveness is like binding a dead body, skin to skin, to a living body. I liken this to a person who refuses to forgive their offender and holds on to past pain and hurt.

Each time you allow yourself to relive the story of your past pain by bringing it up in frequent conversations, this is like carrying around the weight of a dead body. In my own life, people were afraid to approach me because I was carrying the weight of unforgiveness and negativity.

It is impossible to attach something dead to something alive and expect the living to remain alive. As time passes, the decomposing body begins to decay the living body and causes an odor. Naturally, this type of odor, would cause people to avoid this person.

Unforgiveness can also affect one's weight and body chemistry. I have ministered to people whose body odor was affected by their wounded spirit while living in unforgiveness and bitterness. In addition, their facial skin broke out in painful acne, but as healing and deliverance took place, all of this changed, as they forgave their offender and accepted Jesus' love and forgiveness.

Forgiveness can be an excellent weight loss program. When we go through depressing or hard issues, habits of excessive eating may be formed and thus lead into further depression that will often continue into a vicious cycle of unforgiveness. In receiving the spiritual probiotic called Forgiveness, you will be able to apply natural probiotics to assist in getting rid of excess weight.

SECONDHAND UNFORGIVENESS

When my aunt was diagnosed with cancer, the doctor asked her how long had she been smoking? She looked with a question in her eyes and answered saying, "I never smoked a day in my life." But he said, "Your lungs are like a smoker's." My aunt then realized her health was affected by the many years she had been around those who smoked. As I ministered to her, I shared,

> *"In the same way SECONDHAND SMOKE is harmful to one's health, SECONDHAND UNFORGIVENESS is harmful to one's soul."*

In the following testimony, Sonia shares how holding on to secondhand unforgiveness impacted her life and how through God's grace and love she forgave.

***

"As Mom Hurt, I am Hurting"
Testimony by Sonia

My name is Sonia and as a child I loved both my parents, but as life went on, I began to feel the hurt from a broken marriage between my parents. My mom's pain from infidelity in the marriage made me very angry towards my dad.

Someone once defined bitterness as a longstanding degenerated unforgiveness.

This is where I found myself. I was experiencing secondhand unforgiveness but I was unaware. When my mom found out that my dad was committing adultery, the pain became unbearable for her and this pain led to bitterness in her heart and mine. Although the anger was directed towards my dad, I did not know that I was taking on my mom's pains and wounds. I held on to the unforgiveness in my heart for a very long time towards my dad. My heart of bitterness was not only poisoning me, but also others in my life. This bitterness was one of the reasons that led to mistrust in my own marriage which eventually ended in divorce.

"Looking diligently lest any man fail of the grace of God; lest any root of bitterness springing up trouble you, and thereby many be defiled" Hebrew 12:15

The Bible warns us that when bitterness is permitted, it can spill over and defile or affect others. So, bitterness manifested into hatred towards my dad and anger towards my mom for staying with him. I attended a Forgiveness and Restoration teaching which allowed me to realize that I was hurting myself and others as I took on my parents' problem.

Thanks be to God, that I found His Grace and a heart of love to be able to forgive both my parents and I have made the choice to forgive myself as well as my ex-husband. Today I am free from bitterness and unforgiveness. According to John 8:36, **"If the Son therefore shall make you free, ye shall be free indeed"**.

I know, that because of God's grace and goodness, I am truly free.

***

Thank God for the freedom that is found through Christ Jesus!

Another example of secondhand unforgiveness can be seen through my friend, Mary's experience. As she prepared for her father's funeral, she became anxious about seeing her sister. The early memory of her sister not acknowledging their father at their grandmother's funeral, still angered her. Mary felt that by ignoring him, her sister had deliberately disrespected him.

Mary did not realize that she was hurting herself by taking on a wound that belonged to her father. She had taken on secondhand unforgiveness.

Mary asked me, "Do you think I should remind her of this incident?"

The first thing that came to my mind was, **"unresolved past pain can cause present pain"**.

So my advice to her was, "If you are able to discuss it with your sister, without letting her feel judged by you, then it might be an eye opener to some things she was not aware of."

I further explained, that she was holding on to two wounds. One on behalf of her deceased father and the other, towards her sister.

Are you carrying secondhand unforgiveness?

_____

_____

_____

_____

_____

_____

_____

_____

_____

_____

_____

_____

_____

SECONDHAND UNFORGIVENESS CAN BE A SLOW KILLER TO YOUR HEART.

Be careful of becoming so bitter and unforgiving towards anyone. It will affect your life, and it might affect or influence another person's life. Remember, we will all have to give an account to God for everything we do. Ecclesiastes 12:13-14 says, **"Let us hear the conclusion of the whole matter: Fear God and keep his commandments: for this is the whole duty of man. For God shall bring every work into judgment, with every secret thing, whether it be good, or whether it be evil".** So, keep a heart of forgiveness and repent of all sins.

"Confess your faults one to another, and pray one for another, that ye may be healed. The effectual fervent prayer of a righteous man availeth much",
James 5:16

"And be ye kind one to another, tenderhearted, forgiving one another, even as God for Christ's sake hath forgiven you." Ephesians 4:32

"Be ye angry, and sin not: let not the sun go down on your wrath, neither give place to the devil".
Ephesians 4:26-27

CIRCLE OF UNFORGIVENESS

Seek God for comfort concerning your wounded soul, so that you do not end up in a circle of unforgiveness. Don't allow your spirit to be defiled.

What do I mean by the circle of unforgiveness? God hates a slandering tongue; a tongue that spreads mischief (gossip).

The Lord is displeased when we spread rumors or gossip. Miriam and Aaron gossiped about Moses and the consequence was that Miriam was struck with leprosy for her pride and for speaking negative words about Moses and his wife. Both Aaron and Miriam were denied entry into the Promise Land for not yielding to Moses' authority (Numbers 12:1-15).

"The words of a talebearer are as wounds, and they go down into the innermost parts of the belly".
Proverbs 18:8

In addition, gossiping and spreading rumors can create division among the body of Christ. In a church setting, gossip can lead to division within the church, which sometimes causes some members to leave the church and can eventually result in a "church split". It is best that we take our offense to God first, instead of gossiping with family and friends. We can't allow one of God's wounded soldiers to die without restoration.

Forgiveness is not necessarily covering or keeping our mouths shut about the hurt that has been afflicted upon us. But turning an offense into gossip will only enlarge the circle of your repentance and the circle of your forgiveness.

To clarify, there are people with evil intentions, for example, those who want to hurt innocent children. As Luke17:2 *says, "It were better for him that a millstone were hanged about his neck, and he cast into the sea, than that he should offend one of these little ones"* In our warning each other about their evil intentions, we should be careful not to start a circle for gossiping. As we seek justice and protection, we should pray for that person that they too can seek forgiveness which is available through Jesus Christ.

Circle of Unforgiveness and Repentance

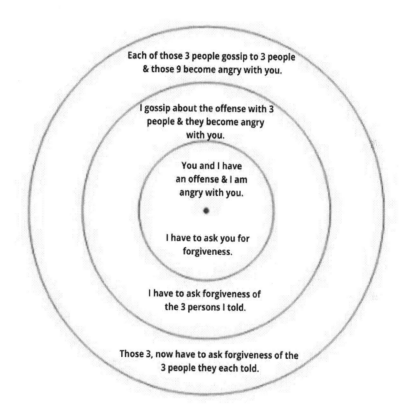

Each of those 3 people gossip to 3 people & those 9 become angry with you.

I gossip about the offense with 3 people & they become angry with you.

You and I have an offense & I am angry with you.

I have to ask you for forgiveness.

I have to ask forgiveness of the 3 persons I told.

Those 3, now have to ask forgiveness of the 3 people they each told.

This is how the circle works.

Beginning at the top of the inner circle.
You do something to offend me and I become angry with you.

Next, move to the top middle circle.
In my anger, I gossip to 3 of my friends about what you have done to offend me. These 3 friends also become angry and resentful towards you. Now, 4 of us are holding unforgiveness.

Lastly, move to the top of the outer circle.
Each of my 3 friends, call 3 of their own friends to tell them of the offense, totaling an additional nine people, carrying second-hand unforgiveness.

To remedy this growing problem, we must choose to forgive our offender, repent for bringing others into our circle of offense and ask for forgiveness.

Let's move to the bottom of the inner circle.
I have to ask for your forgiveness for sharing the offense with others.

Next, move to the bottom middle circle.
I also have to ask my three friends for forgiveness, because I brought them into a place of anger, bitterness and unforgiveness towards you.

Finally, move to the bottom of the outer circle.
My three friends, have to ask forgiveness from each of their friends, whom they gossiped to, which had caused them to walk in anger, bitterness and unforgiveness towards you.

This circle shows how an offense between two people can spread to others. This can be used not just in the case of gossip but in the case of lying, stealing, cheating on a test, having an extramarital affair or more.

Mary gets into an argument with her friend Betty of over 10 years. Mary decides to tell her sister Jane (who is a Christian), about what happened between her and Betty.

As a good sister to Mary, Jane feels that her sister Mary has the right to be offended. So she also takes on the offense and criticizes Betty in a negative way, which is unlike her character. Betty is unaware that she has taken on secondhand unforgiveness (like secondhand smoke).

Mary, now feels bad about what Jane said about Betty.

As the days go by, the Holy Spirit reminds Mary that if she had not spoken of the offense to her sister in a negative way, her sister would not be speaking badly about Betty. 1Timothy 5:22 says, *"...neither be partaker of other men's sins: keep thyself pure"*.

Jane inadvertently took on a heart of secondhand unforgiveness.

So, Mary's Circle of Sin now becomes her Circle of Repentance, as she asks both Betty and her sister for forgiveness.

Matthew 18:15 gives us an example of how to deal with an offense with a brother/sister, *"Moreover if thy brother shall trespass against thee, go and tell him his fault between thee and him alone: if he shall hear thee, thou hast gained thy brother."* One must be careful who they take advice from in these cases. Each person you have pulled into your circle of gossip fostering unforgiveness will need to be approached and asked for their forgiveness because you pulled them into your circle of sin.

Our circle of sin equals our circle of repentance.

There are times when we are reminded by the Holy Spirit that we must revisit this circle to be set free from evil spoken words towards someone else.

CHAPTER SEVEN
"Repentance"

It is important to approach the throne of God with a contrite heart, for without repentance there can be no forgiveness of sin. In addition, be ready to stop repeating the same sins because true repentance does not repeat the act.

Let us take a look at a good background story in the bible of a contrite heart.

In 2 Samuel 12, Nathan the Prophet was sent to David to expose the wrong he did with Bathsheba by committing the sin of adultery, then murdering her husband, Uriah the Hittite.

Nathan spoke in a parable to David and when David heard this parable of one man taking another man's only lamb, in comparison to the fact that he had a herd of sheep, David was very angry of this evil that was done. As David became angry, Nathan pointed out to David that, "You are that man!" David was pointing outward but Nathan had to let him know that he was the one who did this evil. Nathan continued to let David know that the Lord would cause this blood guilt to remain in his bloodline and so it did. David's confrontation with Nathan the Prophet and conviction by God, led to a heart of repentance.

David's fellowship with God was broken, but his relationship with God was still intact. As he acknowledged his sin and repented, his life changed. He became known as a man after God's own heart. David was one of Israel's greatest kings in history.

129

Through his loins, the promise was fulfilled that a seed from David's, a king will arise and will reign on the throne forever. This King is Jesus Christ, the King of all kings, Lord of all lords and Lion of the tribe of Judah.

David's example of a prayer of repentance, leading to forgiveness and restoration is Psalm 51: 1-6.

Have mercy upon me, O God, according to thy lovingkindness: according unto the multitude of thy tender mercies blot out my transgressions. 2 Wash me throughly from mine iniquity, and cleanse me from my sin. 3 For I acknowledge my transgressions: and my sin is ever before me. 4 Against thee, thee only, have I sinned, and done this evil in thy sight: that thou mightest be justified when thou speakest, and be clear when thou judgest. 5 Behold, I was shapen in iniquity; and in sin did my mother conceive me. 6 Behold, thou desirest truth in the inward parts: and in the hidden part thou shalt make me to know wisdom.

When we admit our sin to God and ourselves, and come into an agreement with Him, He will point out our sin, through the leading of the Holy Spirit; this will lead us into true repentance.

We should not try to justify our sin, but ask God to restore His joyful fellowship to us. As He restores the fellowship, we will share and teach others what we have learned about God's Love, forgiveness, restoration, joy and deliverance.

A Testimony of Repentance
By Suzanne Phillippa Marcellus

As a young girl, at the age of seven, I fell in love with Jesus. Although I never saw Him with my eyes or heard Him with my ears, I knew without a doubt that He existed and that He loved me. When I would sing songs in Sunday School and in church, I sang from the depths of my soul. I knew that God could hear every word and He was pleased with me. As a second grader, I would passionately tell girls in the bathroom that they needed to believe in Jesus to be saved.

I also remember the struggles I had as an elementary student, the obsession with masturbation, wanting attention from boys, and using profanity at school. I grew in this unhealthy way of thinking that I could be inside of Jesus and enjoy the pleasures of the sinful nature. Whether or not I knew or understood any better from age 7-10, I don't recall; but I do know my family had no idea about the struggles that I wrestled with and I knew that I had to keep them hidden.

Remember how Adam and Eve hid in the Garden of Eden (Genesis 3:8)? Although they did not have the full understanding of the judgments that would be on them and all mankind, a fear of exposure came over them; that same fear comes over all of us when we sin. The question is, will you come to God on **bended knees and tears** or will you continue in the path that leads you away from Him?

Middle school introduced greater struggles of trying to fit in with my peers, avoid being made fun of because my nose was different than everyone else and being interested in older boys. The difference in elementary school was although I was "boy crazy", I would not dare compromise my body or my lips, but in Middle School, a boy you liked, expected to be kissed. It was a transition from imaginations to realities. All of the boyfriends I had, except for one, were significantly older than me and wanted me to do things with them that girls their age were willing to do, and I would now be taught by them.

In all this, I continued the mixture of my faith in Jesus and my bondage to sin. I would still preach about Jesus, it was like Jeremiah, when He says God's word was like fire shut up in His bones (Jeremiah 20:9). At the age of 13, an eighth grader, I was filled with the Holy Spirit, with the gift of a heavenly prayer language (Jude 1:20). I was so hungry to receive this infilling and the preacher that prayed for me that night said **unforgiveness** blocks you from receiving the Holy Spirit. I had a lot of **unforgiveness** towards two very specific persons in my life, but I wanted God more than I wanted to hate, so at thirteen, **I FORGAVE and I WAS FILLED**.

I went to school the following day overflowing with the love and presence of God. I would speak to my friends and my language would change to the heavenly one I received (Acts 19:6). I did not know how to control or cap the work our Heavenly Father was doing in my life. Now I was spirit-filled and excited about my relationship with God, but the temptations didn't stop, and I did not know how to stop them or overcome them. I wrestled continuously inside of myself.

At 16, a junior in high school, I fell in love with a boy and wanted to spend the rest of my life with him. Since I was a little girl I would always wonder if every boy I thought was cute would become my future husband. I don't know about other girls my age, but I was obsessed with finding my husband, and I was sure I found Him. The summer before this school year began, I promised God my virginity at a Christian camp in North Carolina. My parents bought me a blue sapphire gold promise ring and I was excited about my decision. Meeting this boy changed everything. I wanted to make him happier than anyone else in the universe, including God. I will never forget the day we chose to give our virginity to each other. I whispered a prayer, telling God that I accepted him as my lawfully wedded husband and that God would not consider our actions as sin.

That was October of 1996, from November 1996 to February 1997, I did not see my menstrual cycle. I remember my father asking me if I was having sex, but I told him no. I said to myself if he asks me if I'm making love then I'll say yes, but technically in my mind I had reasoned that what we experienced was more than sex. The time came in February when my mother took me to the gynecologist, concerned that my body was in trouble. She told the doctor, that he was not allowed to give me a pregnancy test because her daughter was not having sex. They gave me the test anyway and the doctor looked at me in the room and said, "How long have you been having sex? You are almost four months pregnant. Do you want to tell your mom or do you want me to?"

Oh the fear, shock and numbness of that day, I will never forget. The pain we caused to both of our families who trusted us completely. The betrayal, shame and disappointment they felt. To this day I believe my father's greatest pain of that moment was that I lied to him about whether we were having sex. The tears I cried in my closet, with my knees close to my chest, all I could sing was, *"Jesus Loves Me"*. It brings tears to my eyes remembering that day. I knew that Jesus would never stop loving me, but I also knew that the pain I caused to the ones I loved was so great and so deep and I couldn't take that pain away.

Years passed and I had many successes in education and in raising my beautiful son with the support of my parents, but I was bound in lust, compromise and sexual sin while trying to serve God. I had lived that way my whole Christian life and although **I had asked God for forgiveness, I never truly repented and turned from sin that so easily entangles.**

I remember the day I went to Mom Cheery at Angel Hair Beauty Salon, as a married woman and mother of two at that time (now I am the mother of four). We were sharing together about repentance and forgiveness. The Lord revealed to me that the pain I caused to my parents at 16 years old is the pain we cause God when we sin against Him. It's important to understand that **Repentance is the sorrow we feel and experience that produces the turning away from sin.** The pain in my Father's eyes reflected the pain in my Heavenly Father's eyes.

The question that we must ask ourselves is, do we really hurt when we hurt God, or do you and I believe

134

that God does not feel the pain of our sin? Do we believe that God is so use to mankind's sin that He has become immune to the pain of adultery against Him? Brothers and sisters, Christ's love is so great and so deep for us that in our love of Him, we must be persuaded not to hurt Him. I guarantee that when we realize that our Heavenly Father is affected by our sin, we will choose to bring Him pleasure by our obedience. If you relate to the pull of the world and God simultaneously producing a compromised walk in Christ, may I encourage you to take a moment and imagine yourself being lied to, betrayed by, cheated on, or abused by someone you love. How do you feel? Do you desire to feel that pain again and again? I don't. Our pain persuades us not to cause that pain to those we love, and no one loves us more than Father God, Jesus our Savior and Precious Holy Spirit.

"Now I am glad I sent it, not because it hurt you, but because the pain caused you to repent and change your ways. It was the kind of sorrow God wants his people to have, so you were not harmed by us in any way. For the kind of sorrow God wants us to experience leads us away from sin and results in salvation. There's no regret for that kind of sorrow. But worldly sorrow, which lacks repentance, results in spiritual death. Just see what this godly sorrow produced in you! Such earnestness, such concern to clear yourselves, such indignation, such alarm, such longing to see me, such zeal, and such a readiness to punish wrong. You showed that you have done everything necessary to make things right."

2 Corinthians 7:9-11

***

This is a good time to praise God for your deliverance, restoration, salvation and His righteousness. After this, make the choice to forgive immediately if you find yourself in a place of woundedness and unforgiveness. This will keep you in tune with the Holy Spirit, humble and broken before God and man. In order to truly forgive, you must be willing to humble yourself. Quick forgiveness and repentance will help one to have an unoffendable heart. In addition, as the peace of God remains in you, ask Him to guard your heart. Philippians 4:7 says, **"And the peace of God, which passeth all understanding, shall keep your hearts and minds through Christ Jesus".**

PRAYER OF REPENTANCE

Examine my heart, Oh Lord, as I repent of the sins of my flesh, my thoughts and my emotions. I repent for the sins of anger, bitterness and all other sins committed consciously and unconsciously. Please forgive me. Transform my heart that is easily offended, which caused unforgiveness to take root in my life. Create in me a clean heart and renew Your right spirit within me. Please do not cast me away from your presence and please don't take your Holy Spirit away from me (Psalm51).

Lord, teach me your ways and guide me in your truth. Help me to become a living sacrifice unto You as your servant. As Jesus served by washing the disciples' feet in humility, teach me how to be a humble servant also in washing others' feet (Mark 10:35-45), and I will teach others Your ways and Your truth. Thank you for forgiving me. I now receive your forgiveness in my life, knowing that the blood of Jesus, cleanses me of all my sins. In Jesus' name, Amen.

CHAPTER EIGHT
"Forgiveness is Not"

Before we discuss what forgiveness is, let's see what forgiveness is not. So, let us follow the example of Christ who when He was rejected, did not fight back, but instead He left vengeance to God His father. Romans 12:19 says, *"Dearly beloved, avenge not yourselves, but rather give place unto wrath: for it is written, Vengeance is mine; I will repay, saith the Lord"*.

Forgiveness helps you to step out of the constant distraction of self-pity. When Nathan the prophet told David that he was wrong for what he did to Uriah, anger arose within him because he knew it was a selfish act. David was distracted and had self-pity because he had no way of reconciling with Uriah. He felt sorry for himself and was praying that he and Bathsheba's child would live.

We need to **forgive ourselves and those who will never be able to return forgiveness as in the case of death.**

Forgiveness must move you out of your comfort zone. As a result, David repented and God forgave and restored him to his original position as King. David is known as a man after God's own heart.

When God forgives us, he chooses to treat us as if it did not happen. Micah 7:19 reminds us that God will cast our sins into the sea of forgetfulness. ***"He will turn again, he will have compassion upon us; he will subdue our iniquities; and thou wilt cast all their sins into the depths of the sea"***.

FORGIVENESS IS NOT...

➢ Forgiveness is **NOT** approval. Jesus forgave the woman caught in adultery, but He didn't approve of her sin; instead He told her to "go and sin no more."(John 8:10-11)

➢ Forgiveness is **NOT** excusing the reason why the offender did what they did to make it easier for them to be forgiven. (Mark 11:25)

➢ Forgiveness is **NOT** pardoning- a legal term meaning "to release from consequences". While you cannot impose your consequences on the offender, you cannot shield them from God's dealing or judgment. (Romans 12:20)

➢ Forgiveness is **NOT** denying or keeping it a secret. Only when we fully acknowledge and come to terms with what was done to us can we truly forgive. (David's story: 2 Samuel 12)

➢ Forgiveness is **NOT** forgetting. It is next to impossible to forget any significant event, but we can *choose* not to allow it to rule our thoughts. Example: I will forgive and allow God to develop my trust. (Ecclesiastes 12:14)

➢ Forgiveness is **NOT** assuming that the offender understands forgiveness. (Matthew 6:14-15)

➢ Forgiveness is **NOT** reconciliation. Reconciliation requires two people to be in agreement to forgive. What if one of them won't agree? (Matthew 18:15-17)

- Forgiveness is **NOT** remaining a victim. (1 Samuel 25:14-32)

- Forgiveness is **NOT** using the word 'but', which is partial forgiveness and total disobedience to God's Word. (1 Samuel 13:7-14)

- Forgiveness is **NOT** rationalizing out the offense in an effort to desensitize yourself. (1 Samuel 15)

- Forgiveness is **NOT** rehashing what was done to you. (2 Samuel 13)

- Forgiveness is **NOT** guilt. Don't allow someone's choice not to forgive you to cause you to walk with guilt. (e.g.) When parents separate or become divorced, children who manipulate with their words can keep a parent or both parents in a place of feeling a false sense of guilt. (2 Samuel 6:16-23)

- Forgiveness is **NOT** a decision to ignore your pain. (Jeremiah 15:18-19)

- Forgiveness is **NOT** condoning that the offense is acceptable.

Long after you think you've forgiven someone, you can still be holding unforgiveness in your heart towards them. You may still feel a nudge in your spirit. You may feel hesitant to trust again. You may experience anger or anxiety when thinking about or seeing the person.

This feeling is uncomfortable, but helps us realize that there is still a wound that needs to be addressed. These are some clues that will help you to know where you are in your life in regards to unforgiveness:

- You get angry thinking about what happened.
- You keep on rehearsing the incident mentally and in conversation.
- You carry an unpleasant attitude towards others.
- You find it hard to trust people.
- You seize every opportunity to remind the offender of what they did, or you resent them.
- You remind others of the hurt that you went through with angry expressions.

When you refuse to forgive, you are basically saying that what Christ has done on the cross, His nail pierced hands and feet, is not enough for you to use as your measure of forgiveness.

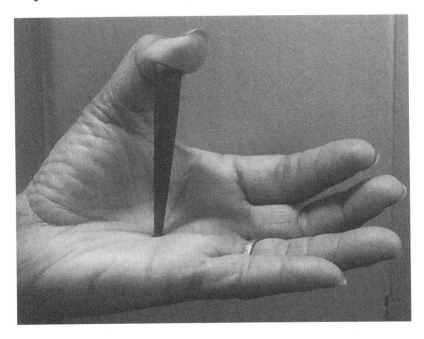

There is no justification to maintain a heart of unforgiveness. This is like trying to take God's authority to get even. Romans 12:19 tells us, "**Dearly beloved, avenge not yourselves, but rather give place unto wrath: for it is written, Vengeance is mine; I will repay, saith the Lord**".

So, the thing to do is let go and let God do what He does best by giving His grace and mercy where it is needed, because He will work it out for your good. Romans 8:28, *"and we know that all things work together form good to them that love God, to them who are the called according to his purpose."*

When people insulted and lied on Jesus, He let God, who is the righteous judge, take care of His cases. When you don't let go of your offender because of unforgiveness you are binding them to you and you become their hostage. This happens when you harbor unforgiveness in your heart, because it can make you **sick**, spiritually and emotionally; **not** the offender.

When you hold on to unforgiveness, it gives the offender control over your life. In addition, holding on to past pain may also cripple your future. Unfortunately, many people are not only still bearing grudge or malice towards person who are alive, but they are also still bearing the grudge or malice towards people who are dead.

Remember, **unforgiveness** looks back, but **forgiveness** looks forward.

Living free is to "stop reliving and start living one day at a time".

Now is the time to forgive, let go and move on. Jesus wants us to live a free life, trusting in Him.

CHAPTER NINE
"Process of Forgiveness"

PROCESS OF FORGIVENESS

People generally have unforgiveness towards God, Self or an Offender. As we go through the process of forgiveness, we must choose to:

☐ Forgive God. We must not hold God accountable for our pains and wounds.

☐ Forgive Yourself.

☐ Forgive your Offender.

☐ Pray for your Offender.

FORGIVE GOD

Jonah held on to his anger towards God and his hatred towards the people of Nineveh to the very end. According to Jonah 4:1-9, Jonah was so outraged and angry that he wanted to die, because the people repented and God forgave them.

God has not sinned against us in any way. When tragic situations occur in our life, we often perceive that God is responsible because He allowed it to happen. The truth is, when bad things happen to us, it hurts God's heart greatly. Therefore, He is not to be blamed for our past or present hurts. God has given every person the free will to make good choices but many times people choose to use this free will to inflict pain and suffering upon themselves and others.

Sometimes, we have hidden anger towards God in our heart. We are blaming Him and asking, "God where were you when I was (abandoned, abused, rejected)_____?"

If you have anger towards God, I encourage you to release it so that you can see His true heart for you. The nature of God includes forgiveness, grace, love and mercy.

Take a minute to search your heart and check if you are carrying any unforgiveness towards God.

_____

_____

_____

Are you ready and willing to stop blaming Him for your pain?

_____

Now join me in this prayer.

Father God,

I choose to release my anger, doubt, disbelief and

_____

towards You. I choose to believe Jeremiah 29:11 which says, *the thoughts and plans you have for me, are to prosper and not harm me, plans to give me a hope and a future.* Now that I know that you are a loving Father who has always had my best interest at heart and that your love for me is so great, I repent of my doubt and for believing that you abandoned me in my moments of hurt and despair, please forgive and heal me, in Jesus name, Amen.

Now, give God thanks for what he has done in forgiving us and setting our wounded heart and spirit free.

"O Lord you searched me and known me you know my sitting down and rising up you understand my thoughts afar off...for there is not a word on my tongue but behold, you know it altogether...I will praise you for I am fearfully and wonderfully made marvelous are your works; and that my soul knoweth right well."
Psalms 139:1-2, 4, 14

FORGIVE YOURSELF

Many times, we are most unforgiving towards ourselves because of situations we have allowed ourselves to go through. Sometimes the pain we experience from past wounds were self-inflicted, like in the case of having an abortion. Other times, as the offender, we carry the guilt of the sin we committed against others. However, God does not want you to hold this charge against yourself. Forgiving yourself frees you to love yourself.

Forgiveness of self, took me back to where it all started. I had to revisit the past to deal with the root

146

cause of my sin, which was jealousy. I reconciled with the nine- year old little girl inside of me so that I could forgive myself. It was only then that I was truly able to accept God's love and forgiveness towards me. This frees me to quickly forgive myself and others, when I offend or others offend me, and allows me not to dwell in the past.

I no longer have pity parties.

Self-forgiveness empowers me to journey forward with God's plans for my life.

> *Reconciling with oneself is an act of receiving God's forgiveness and love.*

We should look in the mirror of our lives and see how Jesus sees us. In having compassion for yourself, it becomes easier to have compassion on others. Since Christ, has forgiven you, knowing all of your flaws and failures, it is time to **choose to forgive yourself**.

"Bless the LORD, O my soul, and forget not all his benefits: 3 Who forgiveth all thine iniquities; who healeth all thy diseases; 4 Who redeemeth thy life from destruction; who crowneth thee with lovingkindness and tender mercies; 5 Who satisfieth thy mouth with good things; so that thy youth is renewed like the eagle's."

Psalm 103:2-5

SELF-FORGIVENESS EXERCISE

Use this prayer and fill in the blank, with those things you need to forgive yourself for and those who have hurt you (i.e. your children, spouse, spiritual leader...)

Father God,

Forgive me for the sins that I have committed towards myself.

I choose to forgive myself for (i.e. abortion, cutting, suicide attempt...)_____

_____

_____

Forgive me for the sins that I have committed against others.

I choose to forgive myself for doubting You about

_____

_____

Forgive me for allowing the actions or words of _____ to put fear in my heart.

☐ I choose to forgive myself for allowing fear to reside in my heart.

Forgive me for allowing the actions or words of _____ to create bitterness in my heart.

☐ I choose to forgive myself for allowing bitterness to reside in my heart.

Forgive me for allowing the actions or words of _____ to create hatred in my heart.

☐ I choose to forgive myself for allowing hatred to reside in my heart.

Forgive me for allowing the actions or words of _____ to hurt me.

☐ I choose to forgive myself for allowing hurt to reside in my heart.

Forgive me for allowing the actions or words of _____ to repeatedly manipulate me.

☐ I choose to forgive myself for allowing others to manipulate me.

Forgive me for self- sabotaging actions that resulted from _____'s actions or words of which stole my innocence.

☐ I choose to forgive myself for holding on to the guilt of something I was not responsible for.

Forgive me for allowing the action or words of _____ to control my emotions.

149

☐ I choose to forgive myself for allowing my emotions to be controlled.

Forgive me for allowing the actions or words of _____to intimidate me.

☐ I choose to forgive myself for allowing myself to be intimidated.

Forgive me for allowing the actions or words of _____to neglect me.

☐ I choose to forgive myself for thinking I deserved to be neglected.

Forgive me for allowing the actions or words of _____to bully me.

☐ I choose to forgive myself for carrying the guilt of allowing myself to be bullied, even though it was not my fault.

Forgive me for allowing the actions or words of _____to create jealousy in my heart.

☐ I choose to forgive myself for allowing myself to be jealous.

Prayer of Self Forgiveness

Lord Jesus,

Please forgive me for allowing my offender to control my emotions and the thoughts that have occupied space in my mind, all of these years. It has prevented me from walking in the fullness of Your plan and divine destiny for my life.

Today I choose to forgive myself and my offender for all the pain I have allowed in my life. Lord, Jesus, I am in agreement with your word, which says: ***For if you forgive men when they sin against you, your heavenly father will also forgive you. But if you do not forgive men their sins, your heavenly father will not forgive your sins.*** " I forgive myself for having unforgiveness in my heart; free me of doubt, anger, resentment, unbelief and bitterness. Thank you dear God, that *"**There is therefore now no condemnation to them which are in Christ Jesus.***" So, I walk in my freedom according to ***John 8:36, which says, who the Son sets free, is free indeed.*** I give you praise, honor and glory for the victory, in setting me free. In the name of Jesus Christ my Savior and Lord, Amen.

Forgiveness is not pretending you were not hurt. It is recognizing that in order to be free, you must release those who have hurt you to God because *"**Hurt** people usually **hurt** other people."*

Have you ever noticed that it is more difficult to forgive your family members? Because of their proximity to us, we expect that they will be the ones to work hard not to hurt us.

Beginning in Genesis 25 we read about two brothers, Jacob and Esau and how Jacob tricked his brother out of his birthright. Esau was very angry to the point of wanting to kill his brother Jacob after he tricked him and their father. Jacob had to leave their home, for his protection. Years later, Jacob and his growing family, journeyed back to his home. To show his repentance, he sent gifts ahead of himself to Esau as a token of being sorry for his past act of unkindness. Esau was elated to see Jacob and his family. Even before Jacob could ask for forgiveness, Esau had already forgiven him.

"And he passed over before them, and bowed himself to the ground seven times, until he came near to his brother. 4 And Esau ran to meet him, and embraced him, and fell on his neck, and kissed him: and they wept." Genesis 33:3-4

"And Jacob said, Nay, I pray thee, if now I have found grace in thy sight, then receive my present at my hand: for therefore I have seen thy face, as though I

had seen the face of God, and thou wast pleased with me." Genesis 33:10

The heart of God is love and forgiveness. In the absence of Jacob, Esau must have realized that by hating his brother he was only hurting himself. Forgiving your offender is one of the greatest acts and gift of love you can give to yourself and others. It can also be one of the hardest things you will ever do, but it's a decision that is worth it. Esau accepted the gifts his brother gave to him. He was eager to see his brother so he could let him know that he had forgiven him.

Is there anything you need to forgive your brother for? Choose to forgive him today.

Father God,

I choose to forgive my brother for _____

_____

1 John 4:20-21 says, *"We love him because he first loved us. If a man says, I love God, and hateth his brother, he is a liar: for he that loveth not his brother whom he hath seen, how can he love God whom he hath not seen? And this commandment have we from him, that he who loveth God love his brother also".*

In Genesis 29 we read of the jealousy between two sisters, Leah and Rachel, who were both Jacob's wives. Laban the women's father had tricked Jacob and gave him Leah as his wife, after Jacob had worked seven years to marry Rachel. You can only imagine what this did to their relationship as sisters

153

and how Leah felt to know she was not loved by Jacob. One week later, Jacob married his love, Rachel, but as time went on, only Leah could have children.

"And when the LORD saw that Leah was hated, he opened her womb: but Rachel was barren."
Genesis 29:31

Rachel was jealous that her sister could have children and Leah was jealous of the love Jacob had towards Rachel.

Sibling rivalry can be birthed out of parents' showing favoritism to one child, because of appearance, gender, talent and more.

Is there anything you need to forgive your sister for? Choose to forgive her today.

Father God,

I choose to forgive my sister for _____

_____

In 2 Samuel 13 we witness the trickery of King David's son, Amnon. Amnon pretended to be sick and asked David to send his sister, Tamar, to care for him, but he raped her. After Absalom waited two years to avenge Amnon by death for violating their sister, he fled for 3 years. By this time, David missed Absalom and wanted to mend the relationship.

"And the soul of king David longed to go forth unto Absalom: for he was comforted concerning Amnon, seeing he was dead."   2 Samuel 13:39

Absalom, however was not in the mood to make up, he wanted to take over is father's throne, and he did.

"And there came a messenger to David, saying, The hearts of the men of Israel are after Absalom. [14] *And David said unto all his servants that were with him at Jerusalem, Arise, and let us flee; for we shall not else escape from Absalom: make speed to depart, lest he overtake us suddenly, and bring evil upon us, and smite the city with the edge of the sword."*
       2 Samuel 15:13-14

Sadly, this story ended with Absalom's death, after he ruled Israel for four years and slept with his father's concubines.

Is there anything you need to forgive your children for? Choose to forgive them today.

Father God,

I choose to forgive my children for _____

_____

Deuteronomy 5:16 says, "Honour thy father and thy mother, as the LORD thy God hath commanded thee; that thy days may be prolonged, and that it may go well with thee, in the land which the LORD thy God giveth thee."

Apology Letter from a
Mother, Grandmother and Aunt

To my Daughter/Son,
Please forgive me for speaking abortion over your life, while you were in my womb. Forgive me for judging you wrongfully and for speaking negative words over your life. Please forgive me for comparing you with what I perceived as your dad's worthlessness and lack of ambition. Forgive me for doubting you and preventing you from going to college because of my religious beliefs at that time. Please forgive me for calling you a liar when you were speaking truth. Forgive me for causing you to have low self-esteem because of my words spoken over you and for saying that you will never get married or amount to anything good. Forgive me for when I spoke domestic violence over your marriage. Please forgive me, my daughter/son.

To my Nephew/Niece,
Please forgive me as an aunt for being jealous towards your progress. Forgive me for not trusting you around my husband. Please forgive me for not believing that my husband molested you. Forgive me for blaming you.

To my Granddaughter/ Grandson,
Please forgive me as a grandmother for not treating you with love and respect and for abusing you. Forgive me for denying you the right to call me Grandma. As a grandmother, you could not trust to tell me that your grandfather molested you, I'm sorry, please forgive me. Forgive me for dragging you to Sunday School, when the teacher was not trustworthy and you tried to tell me. Please forgive

me for ignoring you when you were craving my attention and for chasing you away when you were trying to get me to make something special for you. Forgive me, my granddaughter and grandson for not being a good example of Jesus to you.

To Everyone,
As a Mother, Grandmother, Aunt, sibling, teacher or any female who has been a part of your life, I am asking you for your forgiveness, on behalf of them. I apologize for the wounds that were caused.

Apology Letter from
Father, Grandfather and Uncle
By: Roy Page

Dear Daughter/Son,
I am sorry as your father to speak so many negative words over you - forgive me. As your dad I should be protecting you and loving you wholesomely. Yet still, I molested you as a child, my own daughter, my own son. I am so sorry for the major scar I have caused in your heart, the wound that you are still feeling today from my selfish and disgusting ways. Please forgive me. I can't find the words to say how sorry I am to violate you and ravish you so violently... I am sorry, forgive me. Please find it in your heart to forgive me. I recognize my wrong and I know you are hurting deeply, but I can only tell you I am saddened and so, so sorry for the pain I have put you through.

I am sorry as your dad to treat your sisters and brothers better than you because I thought you were not my child. I am sorry that because you were my step-daughter/step-son I treated you indifferently. I was wrong. Forgive me.

Dear Step-Daughter/Step-Son,
I am sorry for putting you through such horrible abuse. Please forgive me.

Dear Cousin,
I am sorry to steal your joy, your peace, your happiness. I am sorry to have raped and abused you, and for treating you like trash, as though you were nobody. You trusted me as your cousin and I took advantage of you, I am sorry. My heart hurts to know that I took away your innocence as a child. When I

use to touch you inappropriately, coerce you not to tell anyone and threaten you if you should tell, I am really sorry. Forgive me.

Dear Girlfriend/Wife,

I am sorry for saying and doing things you don't like as my wife. For putting you down, for not valuing you, for not appreciating you, for not providing, caring and loving you as I should as your husband. Please forgive me. I am sorry for the burden I placed on you, for the loneliness you have felt because I was never there for you when you needed me most. I am sorry. Sorry for the harsh words I have said to you, sorry I hurt your feelings, sorry for cheating on you. I won't do it again. Forgive me. Let's talk about it. Please open your heart and forgive me.

I am sorry I persuaded you to let your daughter sleep with me because I was your only source of income.
I am sorry for the many abortions I have caused you to do. I am sorry for the innocent blood that I have shed. I am sorry, I have no excuses for pressuring you to do these abortions. Forgive me.

Thank you for not aborting our daughter and son. Look at them now, you have done a great and awesome job with them as a single mother. I pray that you forgive me. I am sorry for mistreating you, for shutting down on you, for not giving you any money to help raise them, for their education. I wasn't around for their birthdays, Christmas, special occasions, like their graduations. I am sorry, and I hope you will be able to forgive me.

Dear Brother/Sister,
Forgive me for lying on you to our parents and for when you use to get all the beatings for the things I did because I was the favorite for our mom and dad. Forgive me.

Dear Mistress,
I am sorry for forcing you to abort our child because I wasn't ready for the child, because I was married. I didn't love you and didn't want anyone to know, because I am a Pastor. As a Pastor, I should know better and be the leader you were looking for. Please forgive me for my sins. I am sorry. How can I make it right? How can I help with your restitution? How can we get restoration? I have realized my injustice, my self-centeredness and have lost my way. I crave your forgiveness, tell me what I can do to make it right and minimize the pain I have put you through?

Dear Friend,
I am sorry as your friend to hurt you. I never knew any better. I am truly sorry. Please forgive me. You confided in me when you were going through issues with your boyfriend/husband and I know you were going through some weak moments and I took advantage and forced myself on you. When you were only needing a friend, a shoulder to cry and lean on, I persuaded you into doing things you wouldn't normally have done. I have disrespected you and our friendship and I am sorry. Forgive me.

Dear Patient,
I am sorry as your Doctor to misdiagnose your child's illness and for prescribing the wrong medications, which has caused your child not to function properly. I am sorry that my misdiagnosis

has cost the life of your child and loved ones. Please forgive me. I am truly sorry for the tears, pain and death I have caused.

Father God, in the name of Jesus, thank you that you have forgiven me for the wrongs that I have caused all these men and women, the pain, the hurt, the agony, the innocence I have taken from them, the abuse I have caused, the deep wounds that are still resonating in their hearts and minds. These are your beautiful creations that I violated with such selfish and self-centeredness and I know it hurts you, too. But, Father, I come to you and give you thanks for Jesus' precious blood that has washed me and these ladies and gentleman from all our sins. I pray that you will reach deeper into these persons hearts and minds, and help them to forgive me and other men like me so they can be restored and set free from the wrong that we as men have caused these beautiful gems that you have given us, to love, cherish and protect, but we foolishly take them for granted and used, abused and misused them. Father, as men, we are sorry. Help these persons to forgive us as we forgive ourselves, in Jesus name, Amen.

Real forgiveness is a lifelong commitment and decision one makes by faith to obey God's Word and to live a lifestyle pleasing to God, growing in intimacy with Him.

Forgiveness is a gift given to us by God, which we give to those we think do not deserve it. In Acts 7, as Stephen was being stoned to death, he being full of the Holy Spirit, gazed into heaven, and saw the Glory of God with Jesus standing at the right-hand side of God. He pleaded with the Lord to forgive his accusers (Acts 7:54-60), yet the cheers of the people, only encouraged Saul to continue to search for Christians to persecute them.

In Acts 9, Saul had an encounter with Jesus and received forgiveness of his sins. The Lord changed his name to Paul. He went on to become one of the leading Apostles and authored most of the books in the New Testament.

When we have a heart of forgiveness, we are able to gaze into the glory of God, just as Stephen did and be filled with the Holy Spirit.

Forgiveness will hurt, but it hurts even more to stay in bondage.

Forgiveness does not mean you will have to trust the person again. For example, if someone has stolen your money or has raped you, your past experience will allow you to be more aware of similar situations. Trust will come as change in that person's character is made evident. We can trust God because we know His character is love according to 1 John 4:8-10,

"He that loveth not knoweth not God; for God is love. ⁹ In this was manifested the love of God toward us, because that God sent his only begotten Son into the world, that we might live through him. ¹⁰ Herein is love, not that we loved God, but that he loved us, and sent his Son to be the propitiation for our sins."

You know you have forgiven a person when you can see them as God sees them and be able to pray a blessing over their soul.

Forgiveness is the glue that repairs broken relationships.

Forgiveness allows God to move on your behalf and will free you from bondage to continue growing in the Lord. You will become the man or woman of God walking in your original destiny. In Matthew 26:50 Jesus called Judas friend when he was about to betray Him.

Mathew 5:22 says, "but I say unto you that whosoever is angry with his brother without a cause shall be in danger of judgement."

"Therefore if thou bring thy gift to the altar, and there rememberest that thy brother hath ought against thee; leave there thy gift before the altar, and go thy way; first be reconciled to thy brother, and then come and offer thy gift."   Matthew 5:23-24
"Then said Jesus, Father, forgive them; for they know not what they do. And they parted his raiment and cast lots."   Luke 23:34

"For if ye forgive men their trespasses, your heavenly Father will also forgive you: But if ye forgive not men their trespasses, neither will your Father forgive your trespasses,"   Matthew 6:14 & 15

So we should be mindful when we are praying and asking God to forgive us, *"And forgive us of our debts, as we forgive our debtors."*   Mathew 6:12

Having unforgiveness towards the living is difficult, but it can be even more difficult when you carry unforgiveness towards the dead. Remember that the grave cannot speak, so even though the person that hurt you is dead, holding on to the unforgiveness can still be harmful to you. Unfortunately, the dead person cannot come back and apologize for the hurt they caused in your life. By all means, you must choose to forgive by faith, so that you can receive full forgiveness from God. I encourage you to pray a blessing over the surviving offspring of your offender.

Use the following prayer as a guide to forgive your offender who is deceased.

Father God, thank you for this opportunity to make the choice to forgive and set my heart free. This day I choose to forgive (grandparent, parent, sibling...)

_____.

Please forgive me for holding on to this offense. I ask you to bless his/her family and their offspring. In Jesus name, Amen.

Ask God to forgive and bless your offender, as well as to convict them to have a repentant/contrite heart.

You will then feel the weight of unforgiveness lifted as forgiveness transforms your heart of stone to a heart of flesh. At this point, if you choose to you can always tell the person all that they did or said that offended you. Be honest with yourself because it is the only way to have freedom within your spirit. As you choose to forgive, you should also ask God to forgive them and to forgive you. It is important to believe and receive God's forgiveness and replace this heart of unforgiveness with God's promise.

Asking God to forgive and bless your offender

Pray asking God to forgive them for the ways they have hurt you.

Bless them! After you have forgiven the individual, it is important to also pray a blessing over them. This blessing releases your heart of the grudge and unforgiveness.

Luke 6:28 tells us to bless those who curse us, and pray for those who mistreat us.

***

Justine Clarke's Testimony

I attended a virtual Zoom Forgiveness Seminar hosted by Pastor Cheery Williams where forgiveness and the effect of forgiving both positive and negative was being discussed.

During the seminar, I began to reflect on my own journey with forgiveness. I recall being in my apartment in early April trying to spend time with God, trying to connect but to no avail and then really clearly feeling the Holy Spirit saying, "Give it to me. You are holding on to hurt and that is not what I desire."

In those quiet hours of the evening I really understood what it felt like to fight with God. (I didn't win but I tried). I pouted, had a tantrum and cried because, quite frankly, I did not want to do what God was asking, which was to reach out to the person who had hurt me and pray for them.

I knew I had every right to be upset...I knew I had every right to be hurt... I truly felt I had every right to refuse.

In that moment, I felt the spirit prodding, "Yes you know in your own understanding, but you do not know what I know and my thoughts are not your thoughts."

It was interesting! I did not feel as if my feelings were being invalidated by the Holy Spirit. To the contrary, it seemed clear that God was stating, "Yes and in

166

spite of that, I want you to acknowledge my will in this moment and willingly forgive."

"Acknowledge your will? I am not going against your will," I thought.

"Aren't you Justine? In judging whether the person is worthy of your forgiveness, once again, are you not deciding in your own understanding, are you not willingly choosing your will to succeed? Tell me Justine, what do you mean when you ask for My will to be done?"

Just like that, a light bulb moment and what forgiveness truly is was revealed to me.

Forgiveness is a journey, but as I have started to read and really meditate on every word, I realized that as a Christian I had so nonchalantly thrown around scriptures without truly pondering the meaning. Pondering whether I was willing to convey them. Saying the Lord's prayer with no hesitation, not acknowledging that in that prayer I pray for God's will to take precedent. In that moment, God showed me that to truly mean the words I pray in the Lord's prayer or the verse (Proverbs 3:5-6), it would always require action as "faith without works is dead" as found in James 2:26

God was asking me to reach out to the person who had hurt me. He was really saying, "Even in the hurt, do you mean it, will you mean it when you say, let My will be done? Even when it makes no sense, and you have every right, will you readily let my will take precedence and forgive?"

This is a journey that I still find myself on, but now I travel this path and do this work with a renewed purpose and vision for why. I, Justine Clarke, choose to stand on the word of God so it may be a light unto my path and to trust in the Lord with all of my heart and to lean not on my own understanding instead in all my ways acknowledging Yahweh that He may direct my path. And that is a promise to myself and God that I have every intention of keeping and allowing nothing, not even the temptation of unforgiveness, bitterness, or grudges to keep me from walking in God's will for my life.

***

Charlene Watson's Testimony

All of my life I've struggled with forgiving others. I used to hold on to grudges and often relive the pain of past hurt. My simple prayer was, "Lord, help me to forgive and let go". But no matter how much I prayed that prayer, I found that I would still be reliving past hurt. I would often listen to preachers and motivational speakers saying "Let it go. Move on". But still I struggled.

It wasn't until Winsome's Forgiveness Workshop that I started to let go. I listened as she spoke about drinking from the cup of poison and *oh how* it rang home. I smiled to myself when she spoke about wishing death upon her ex-husband and thought to myself, "but this is just like me". At the time when I wished death upon my child's father, it wasn't so much about material gain but more of wanting to be free from him and the abuse (physical, verbal, emotional). I wished death on him because I didn't want to commit the act myself. I didn't want my sins to follow my son. I had thought of ways to kill him.

At the end of this meeting, Roy Page prayed and apologized on behalf of the men. I cried real tears as I received this prayer and apology. I literally felt like a weight was lifted from my heart and I knew then and there that I was ready to forgive my son's father for all the hurt, pain and betrayal. Until Winsome mentioned that she went to her ex-husband and apologized, I didn't think that I needed to apologize for anything. After all, I was the one that was hurt by him. I then took a stock of my time with my son's father and admitted to myself that I wasn't always the saint. I did and said hurtful things to him and conceded that I needed to apologize, too.

Leaving the meeting that night led me to a lot of introspection and self-assessment; this I continue to do frequently. I'm not sure if that was the night that I made a list of the persons that I wanted to forgive or ask for their forgiveness, but somewhere along the journey I made a list. At the top of the list was my name. My childhood wasn't exactly the best and for a long time I struggled with self-esteem issues and self-loathing, so much so that I was suicidal at age 11.

On my list, were some persons who were dead, including my father, my grand aunt (whom I grew up with) and my son's father, amongst some other persons. I knew that I couldn't reach the dead, but since the passing of my father in 2017, I've always wished that he was still alive, so that my son would get to know him. (This wish could be because my son's father is absent, I don't know). Back in 2017, I wasn't even thinking about forgiving him or anything like that. I was just thinking that it would've been nice for my son to know his grandfather.
Coming from the meeting on August 9th, I wrote three letters, one to myself and the other two to my father and my grand aunt. In the letter to myself I apologized and asked myself for forgiveness. I wrote, "I set me free" and that "1 love me" (sounds crazy?).

In the letter to my father, I wrote that I forgave him for not being there as a father should and went on to forgive him for not providing for my two little sisters (whose mother had died). I apologized for hating him and not trying to connect with him after we reunited.

170

My grand aunt's letter was much of the same, saying that I forgave her and I apologized for lying and stealing from her and being the difficult child that I was. Oddly, at the end of those letters I somehow felt lighter and happier in my heart.

I knew that I had to forgive my son's father and apologize to him too. But I had questions about the method I should use to communicate with him. I wrote the letter to him, thought of calling him or sending an e-mail or text. I sat with these questions for a few days and even prayed for God to give me the courage to make the phone call, but I never did. After speaking to Winsome, I have since sent the email to my son's father and know in my heart of hearts that I truly forgive him for real this time and that our soul tie has been broken.

***

Jesus said in John 6:63, *"It is the spirit that quickeneth; the flesh profiteth nothing: the words that I speak unto you, they are spirit, and they are life"*. Therefore, let forgiveness become a part of your lifestyle, choose to forgive immediately.

Begin to speak life over yourself, other people and your situations. Proverbs 18:21 teaches, *"Death and life are in the power of the tongue: and they that love it shall eat the fruit thereof."*

CHAPTER TEN
"Applying Forgiveness"

In Genesis 50:15-21, we read about the life of Joseph. His dreams and the favor of their father, caused his brothers to hate him, to the point of selling him into slavery. Joseph had enough reasons to dislike and have unforgiveness towards his brothers for what they had done to him. Because of their painful actions, he found himself in Potiphar's palace and while there, he was being enticed by Potiphar's wife who was trying to lead him in sexual sin against God. He was imprisoned for a number of years because he rejected Potiphar's wife's offer.

Despite the problems that Joseph was faced, he still had faith and hope in the promises of God. His faith became a reality when Pharaoh had a dream that only Joseph could interpret. Pharaoh told Joseph that God had made the interpretation known to him and that there was no one wiser and with more understanding as him. He then put Joseph in charge of his palace and commanded all of Egypt to obey Joseph's orders.

(Side note: Your gift can make room and provision for you as Joseph's interpretation of dreams made room for him).

As the years went by, Pharaoh's dream came to pass. The famine was severe throughout Egypt and its neighboring countries, including Canaan. This brought many people to Egypt, looking for food, including Joseph's brothers. Joseph recognized his brothers amongst all the foreigners. Although he had great power in Egypt and could have used this authority to kill or take revenge on them, for the physical and emotional wounds they afflicted on him, he did not.

The Apostle Paul urges us in Romans 12:19, **"Dearly beloved, avenge not yourselves, but rather give place unto wrath: for it is written, Vengeance is mine; I will repay, saith the Lord"**.

Joseph revealed himself to his brothers and set them free from their fears. Since Joseph's brothers used their dad as protection from Joseph, when their father died, they were worried Joseph would pay them back for the things they had done to him.

Genesis 50:15-20 records, *"And when Joseph's brethren saw that their father was dead, they said, Joseph will peradventure hate us, and will certainly requite us all the evil which we did unto him. 16 And they sent a messenger unto Joseph, saying, Thy father did command before he died, saying, 17 So shall ye say unto Joseph, Forgive, I pray thee now, the trespass of thy brethren, and their sin; for they did unto thee evil: and now, we pray thee, forgive the trespass of the servants of the God of thy father. And Joseph wept when they spake unto him. 18 And his brethren also went and fell down before his face; and they said, Behold, we be thy servants. 19 And Joseph said unto them, Fear not: for am I in the place of God? 20 But as for you, ye thought evil against me; but God meant it unto good, to bring to pass, as it is this day, to save much people alive. 21 Now therefore fear ye not: I will nourish you, and your little ones. And he comforted them, and spake kindly unto them."*

Although Joseph had more than enough reasons to despise his brothers and hold on to unforgiveness, he forgave his brothers and clearly let them know that what they had meant for evil, God turned it around for the many who could be saved.

> **Salvation can come out of an act of forgiveness.**

This is a good time to ask Holy Spirit to bring to your remembrance those you need to forgive and those who need to forgive you. Be willing to set aside time alone in the presence of the Lord so that you are better able to discern and focus on His voice.

As He speaks in that still small voice, make note of any names or events that are brought back to your remembrance. As He reminds you of any offense(s), it is important to evaluate the condition of your heart to see if there are any pains or wounds that you are still nurturing. Revisit the lists you compiled in Chapters 3, 4 and 5 and choose to forgive your offenders. Make notes where applicable.

Ask the Lord to give you the desire and the faith to forgive. We have all the tools we need to forgive. We only need to determine to make the choice to do it. Be willing to deal with the offense immediately, aggressively and truthfully. Once you have dealt with the most painful experiences, it will be easier to deal with smaller areas of unforgiveness in your heart.

Your offender(s) may be:
- ☐ God
- ☐ Friends
- ☐ Pastor/Church Family
- ☐ Political Leaders
- ☐ Relatives
  - ○ Cousin
  - ○ Father/Mother
  - ○ Grandfather/Grandmother
  - ○ Husband/Wife
  - ○ Brother/Sister
  - ○ Aunt/Uncle
  - ○ Daughter/Son
- ☐ Self
- ☐ Teacher

After you have become aware of those you need to forgive, make the choice to declare (speak) out loud that you have forgiven the offender(s) or those who you have offended. It is important to state that you choose to forgive them.

We don't forgive because the person deserves it. We do, so that we can live a life of forgiveness. As you do, Holy Spirit will minister hope and freedom. Romans 8:2 states, *"For the law of the Spirit of life in Christ Jesus hath made me free from the law of sin and death."*

FORGIVENESS ROLE-PLAYS

1. You can place a picture of the person on a wall.
2. Stand in front of an empty chair and pretend that person you are asking for their forgiveness/or forgiving is sitting on the chair.
3. Ask someone you trust to stand as a representative for the person who offended you (or who you have offended) and speak out to them for the things you are declaring forgiveness.

After choosing one of the above role-play, call your offender by name and remind them briefly of what they did or said to you that was offensive, letting them know that you now choose to forgive them.

Some of the offenses that may have been committed are:

- [ ] Abandonment
- [ ] Adultery
- [ ] Lack of Culture Sensitivity
- [ ] Lack of Empathy
- [ ] False Doctor's Report
- [ ] False Prophecy/Teaching(s)/Doctrine
- [ ] Gossip
- [ ] Hatred
- [ ] Jealousy/Envy of achievements or success
- [ ] Verbal Abuse/Negative Spoken Words
- [ ] Emotional/Mental Abuse
- [ ] Physical Abuse
- [ ] Manipulation and Control
- [ ] Molestation/Rape
- [ ] Racism
- [ ] Rejection
- [ ] Stealing

- [ ] Disrespect
- [ ] Disobedience
- [ ] Murder

Some of the results of the offenses may be:
- [ ] Change of body chemistry.
- [ ] Death
- [ ] Depression
- [ ] Divorce
- [ ] Low Self-Esteem.
- [ ] Lack of Self-Confidence.
- [ ] Poverty
- [ ] Sickness
- [ ] You begin to hurt/wound others.

Here is a general example of what you could say to your offender:

(Fill in the offended / offender's name) and say,

"I choose to forgive you for all the hurt and disappointment you have caused me, when you: (Fill in the offense).

"I choose to forgive you for controlling my emotions."

"I choose to forgive you for causing me to hurt others, using the same afflictions that you used to hurt me."

"I choose to forgive you and release you of these charges."

Here is an example, which includes things that adult children and young children have had to say to their parents:

Mom, I choose to forgive you for telling me that you should have sat on me during the time of my birth.

Dad/Mom, I choose to forgive you for planting negative seeds in my thoughts that I lived out, because I began to believe the lies that I have no value, which almost destroyed me.

Dad/Mom, I choose to forgive you for manipulating me and calling it love.

Dad/Mom, I choose to forgive you for being angry with me without any fault of my own, which caused me to eat excessively.

Dad/Mom, I choose to forgive you for putting fear of traveling on mission trips overseas, as the Lord was leading me.

Dad/Mom, I choose to forgive you for not showing me genuine love, which hindered me from receiving genuine love from others.

Dad/Mom, I choose to forgive you for I have allowed you to cause me to carry this wound in my marriage and parenting, so I am asking you to forgive me.

Mom, I choose to forgive you for the many times you said to me that you wanted a boy instead of a girl because you believe boys are closer to their moms.

<u>Mom</u>, I choose to forgive you for saying that I'm just like my "unreliable and worthless" dad.

<u>Dad/Mom</u>, I choose to forgive you for all the harsh words you have spoken over my life. For example, saying that I had a prostitution spirit, calling me dirty and junkie.

<u>Mom</u>, I choose to forgive you for envying the relationship I have with my father and even my husband. I forgive you, because I know it was difficult for you to understand me not telling you that I was molested by my step-father.

<u>Dad/Mom</u>, I choose to forgive you for you not trying to understand who I am in Christ Jesus.

<u>Dad/Mom</u>, I choose to forgive you for thinking that you knew what was best for my life when you gave me away to my grandmother at three years old.

<u>Dad/Mom</u>, I choose to forgive you for touching me inappropriately as a child.

<u>Dad/Mom</u>, I choose to forgive you for trusting the pastor's words instead of mine after he molested me.

<u>Dad/Mom</u>, I choose to forgive you for giving me to the man that raped me.

Now that you have acknowledged your pain and confronted and chosen to forgive your offender(s) in person or by role play, say the following prayer.

FORGIVENESS PRAYER

By: Herb and Michelle Warden

Father in the name of Jesus, I thank you that while I was yet a sinner, Jesus died the most gruesome death for me. You didn't wait for me to ask for forgiveness. You didn't wait until I straightened out my life. You extended mercy to me, by loving me when I deserved punishment and you released unending grace upon my life, rewarding me with heaven and a relationship with You in exchange for my sin and shame. In forgiving me, setting me free and inviting me into your kingdom, you demonstrated a love that moved you to act on my behalf. Today, as your child, your love moves me into action through forgiving (say the name(s) of those you forgive).

First, I repent of the sin of unforgiveness. I turn from harboring any resentment, bitterness, anger, or ill-will against (say the name(s) of those you forgive). Thank you for forgiving me of this sin. Holy Spirit, please help me to see clearly when unforgiveness attempts to make a home in my heart again.

In the authority of the name of Jesus, and as a joint heir with Him, carrying His name, I rebuke any unforgiveness I've allowed into my temple. In Jesus name I command you to leave! You have no legal access to me anymore. I shut the door to you in Jesus Name!

Father, thank you for giving me the opportunity and heart to forgive (say the name(s) of those you forgive). Thank you for removing the weight of unforgiveness that I have been carrying. I am a carrier of the mercy you show me every day and in shedding this unforgiveness, I'm reminded that you love me dearly.

In Jesus name, Amen.

How do you feel?

_____

_____

_____

_____

_____

_____

Doesn't it feel much lighter now, that you have released your offender?

_____

_____

_____

_____

_____

_____

Use the following worksheets as a guide to list the name(s) of your offender(s) and the offenses that you are releasing. The final step is to pray for those who have wounded you.

Forgiving Your Offender

_____,
I choose to forgive you, for all the hurt and disappointment you caused me when you:

_____

_____

_____

I choose to forgive you for controlling my emotions by:

_____

_____

_____

I choose to forgive you for causing me to hurt others, using the same afflictions that you used to hurt me.

I choose to forgive and release you of these charges.

Father God,
Thank you for this opportunity to make the choice to forgive and set my heart free. Your Word says, no one comes to You, unless You draw them. This day as I forgive_____, I ask that you would soften his/her heart, draw him/her into your salvation, and not hold this charge against him/her. Please care for, bless and forgive_____, his/her children and extended family.
In Jesus name, Amen.

Forgiving Your Offender

_____,
I choose to forgive you, for all the hurt and disappointment you caused me when you:

_____

_____

_____

I choose to forgive you for controlling my emotions by:

_____

_____

_____

I choose to forgive you for causing me to hurt others, using the same afflictions that you used to hurt me.

I choose to forgive and release you of these charges.

Father God,
Thank you for this opportunity to make the choice to forgive and set my heart free. Your Word says, no one comes to You, unless You draw them. This day as I forgive_____, I ask that you would soften his/her heart, draw him/her into your salvation, and not hold this charge against him/her. Please care for, bless and forgive_____, his/her children and extended family.

In Jesus name, Amen.

Forgiving Your Offender

_____,
I choose to forgive you, for all the hurt and disappointment you caused me when you:

_____

_____

_____

I choose to forgive you for controlling my emotions by:

_____

_____

_____

I choose to forgive you for causing me to hurt others, using the same afflictions that you used to hurt me.

I choose to forgive and release you of these charges.

Father God,
Thank you for this opportunity to make the choice to forgive and set my heart free. Your Word says, no one comes to You, unless You draw them. This day as I forgive_____, I ask that you would soften his/her heart, draw him/her into your salvation, and not hold this charge against him/her. Please care for, bless and forgive_____,
his/her children and extended family.

> In Jesus name, Amen.

Forgiving Your Offender

_____

I choose to forgive you, for all the hurt and disappointment you caused me when you:

_____

_____

_____

I choose to forgive you for controlling my emotions by:

_____

_____

_____

I choose to forgive you for causing me to hurt others, using the same afflictions that you used to hurt me.

I choose to forgive and release you of these charges.

Father God,
Thank you for this opportunity to make the choice to forgive and set my heart free. Your Word says, no one comes to You, unless You draw them. This day as I forgive_____, I ask that you would soften his/her heart, draw him/her into your salvation, and not hold this charge against him/her. Please care for, bless and forgive_____, his/her children and extended family.

In Jesus name, Amen.

I know that the previous exercise was difficult. I pray that the Lord comforts you as we continue on this journey.

I was able to forgive my father for committing adultery when I met five of my siblings that weren't my mother's children. We were able to talk and share what took place in our different homes with our dad and our mothers. An amazing thing happened, one brother asked, *"Is it ok to call you Aunty Cheery?"* With a smile I answered, *"Yes."*

With a great big smile, one sister asked, *"I feel comfortable with you, can I call you, Mamma Cheery".* With joy and awe, I said, *"Sure".*

My heart was overwhelmed with passion when one brother asked, *"Sis, can I call you Dad? Meeting you and looking in your face, feels like I am looking and talking to our dad.* So I represented on behalf of our dad and asked my brother, as a father to forgive me for all the pain our father had caused him. He responded, *"This has allowed me to forgive our dad and myself for holding on to anger and unforgiveness because of the abandonment, rejection and all other wounds that have affected me over the years."*

PRAISE GOD!
YOU HAVE CHOSEN TO
FREE YOURSELF FROM BONDAGE!

In the past, you held on to your offender, perhaps thinking you knew how to punish them better than God. Today you have chosen to trust God to deal justly with your offender, in a way that will make them rethink their actions.

YOU HAVE FORGIVEN YOURSELF AND YOUR OFFENDER(S)!

Continue to allow the Lord to work in your life. He is our ultimate example of how to forgive sin.

YOU HAVE CHOSEN NOT TO TAKE VENGEANCE IN YOUR OWN HANDS!

"Dearly beloved, avenge not yourselves, but rather give place unto wrath: for it is written, Vengeance is mine; I will repay, 'saith the Lord;'"   Romans 12:19

Here are some scriptures you can pray after dealing with unforgiveness.

"Create in me a clean heart, O God! And renew a right spirit within me. Restore unto me the joy of thy salvation and uphold with thy free spirit;"
Psalm 51:10 & 12

"If the Son therefore shall make you free, ye shall be free indeed"   John 8:36

"Put on therefore, as the elect of God, holy and beloved, bowels of mercies, kindness, humbleness of mind, meekness, longsuffering; forbearing one another, and forgiving one another, if any man have a quarrel against any: even as Christ forgave you, so also do ye. And above all these things put on charity, which is the bond of perfectness. And let the peace of God rule in your hearts, to the which also ye are called in one body; and be ye, thankful. Let the word of Christ dwell in you richly in all wisdom; teaching and admonishing one another in psalms and hymns and spiritual songs, singing with grace in your hearts

to the Lord. And whatsoever ye do in word or deed, do all in the name of the Lord Jesus, giving thanks to God and the Father by him."   Colossians 3:12-17

"To appoint unto them that mourn in Zion, to give unto them beauty for ashes, the oil of joy for mourning, the garment of praise for the spirit of heaviness; that they might be called trees of righteousness, the planting of the LORD, *that he might be glorified."*   Isaiah 61:3

"But the scripture hath concluded all under sin that the promise by faith of Jesus Christ might be given to them that believe. But before faith came, we were kept under the law, shut up unto the faith which should afterwards be revealed."   Galatians 3:22-23

"Bow down thine ear, O LORD, *hear me: for I am poor and needy. Preserve my soul; for I am holy: O thou my God, save thy servant that trusteth in thee. Be merciful unto me, O Lord: for I cry unto thee daily. Rejoice the soul of thy servant: for unto thee, O Lord, do I lift up my soul. For thou, Lord, art good, and ready to forgive; and plenteous in mercy unto all them that call upon thee."*   Psalms 86:1-5

"For though he was crucified through weakness, yet he liveth by the power of God. For we also are weak in him, but we shall live with him by the power of God toward you. Examine yourselves, whether ye be in the faith; prove your own selves. Know ye not your own selves, how that Jesus Christ is in you, except ye be reprobates? But I trust that ye shall know that we are not reprobates. Now I pray to God that ye do no evil; not that we should appear approved, but that ye should do that which is honest, though we be as reprobates".   2 Corinthians 13:4-7

The Lord's Prayer

"After this manner, therefore pray ye: "Our Father which art in heaven, Hallowed be thy name, Thy kingdom come, Thy will be done, in earth, as it is in heaven. Give us this day our daily bread. And forgive us our debts, as we forgive our debtors. And lead us not into temptation, but deliver us from evil: For thine is the kingdom, and the power and the glory, forever and ever. Amen" Matthew 6:9-13

CHAPTER ELEVEN
"Healing and Restoration"

Even though it is necessary to forgive, forgiveness by itself will not completely heal a wounded spirit. Forgiveness deals with making our hearts right before God. In previous chapters we identified soul wounds that have been caused through emotional, physical or spiritual offenses. God is the only restorer of all wounds. He wants us to live a wholesome physical and spiritual life. Jeremiah 30:17 says, ***"For I will restore health unto thee, and I will heal thee of thy wounds, saith the Lord;"***

No matter what has happened in your past, God's plan is to bring you to a place where the negative issues of the past will no longer affect your present or future life in Christ Jesus. God's Word promises to restore the fullness of our lives.

Imagine yourself as a plant and your offenders as the organisms that work together to destroy plants. In Joel 2:25 there are four types of destroyers mentioned: the locust, the cankerworm, the caterpillar and the palmerworm. All four organisms will eat away at the leaf, the branch, the main stalk and finally the root. At the end, the plant will be destroyed.

Likewise, the enemy will use those around us to eat away at our thoughts, which negatively impact our words, and results in a negative change in our actions, ultimately destroying our reputation.

Types of Organisms	Types of Wounds
Locusts	Thoughts Your negative thoughts of me, hurt me and I begin to believe that I am who you think I am.
Cankerworms	Words Your negative words, hurt me, and I begin to believe they are true.
Caterpillars	Actions Your negative actions towards me, hurt me, and I begin to believe that I deserve to be treated that way.
Palmerworms	Reputation I allow your insults of my character to define me.

"And I will restore to you the years that the locust hath eaten, the cankerworms and the caterpillars and palmerworms, my great army which I sent among you." Joel 2:25

God wants to restore your thoughts, words, actions and reputation. Are you ready to deal with your wounds so they will not infect you any longer? You will know that wounds are present, because they come with a reminder of pain. In this chapter we will invite Jesus to help us process our hurt so that we can be healed and renewed. The Father's heart's desire is to keep our souls clean from infectious wounds.

The objective of healing our wounded soul is not to dig up "old bones or old wounds", nevertheless it is necessary to revisit the root that caused the wound, but we should not plan to live there.

Revisiting our wounded place may be a challenge but it is necessary for our healing. In doing so, we will identify if we were or were not at fault.

If you are the offender, ask the Lord to open your eyes and heart to the wrong you have done and repent of it (Psalms 51). Remember, our God is a loving father who is ready to forgive us of all our sins when we repent (Matthew 6: 9-15).

God is able and willing to restore us regardless of our mistakes or the ways in which we are wounded. We all have a past of good and bad memories that affect our lives today. Restoration of our heart occurs when we make the decision to forgive. With God all things are possible. He has already paid the price for our sins and wounds through His death, burial and resurrection, we only have to believe.

"And we have known and believed the love that God hath to us. God is love; and he that dwelleth in love dwelleth in God and God in him."

1 John 4:16

Isaiah 1:5-6 describes the wounded,

"Why should you be beaten anymore? Why do you persist in rebellion? Your whole head is injured, your whole heart afflicted. From the sole of your foot to the top of your head there is no soundness—only wounds and welts and open sores, not cleansed or bandaged or soothed with oil.

When the Lord spoke of Israel's wounds, He was not speaking of physical wounds but spiritual wounds caused by the sin of idolatry. Wounds are inflicted when sin is present, so whether you sin or someone sins against you, a wound may be inflicted. In the case of being stabbed, the one who is stabbed is the victim. It does not only affect him/her physically but creates an emotional wound.

Jeremiah 8:18-22 also speaks of Israel's wounds,

"When I would comfort myself against sorrow, my heart is faint in me. 19 Behold the voice of the cry of the daughter of my people because of them that dwell in a far country: Is not the LORD in Zion? Is not her king in her? Why have they provoked me to anger with their graven images, and with strange vanities? 20 The harvest is past, the summer is ended, and we are not saved. 21 For the hurt of the daughter of my people am I hurt; I am black; astonishment hath taken hold on me. 22 Is there no balm in Gilead; is there no physician there? Why then is not the health of the daughter of my people recovered?"

194

The Lord had seen their sinful state and the wounds that occurred as a result of their sins, so Jeremiah asked, **"Is there no balm in Gilead; is there no physician there?"**

Balm was a mixture of herbs applied to a wound in that time. Gilead was a fertile region South East of the Sea of Galilee where they would pick these herbs for the care of the wound(s). In my travel to Israel, it was a pleasure to see rosemary and many other healing herbs grow wild along the highway or main roads.

The healing herbs were available for the physical wounds of the children of Israel, so Jeremiah in essence, was asking, "Is there no balm for his people's spiritual wounds?" God was their source of healing and He is still our source of healing. He is our Great Physician. Through Jesus' death on the cross, burial and resurrection we can be healed and set free. The greatest healing is available to us through the shed blood of Jesus Christ, who heals, saves, redeems and delivers us, giving us the ministry of reconciliation.

Isaiah 61:1 is quoted by Jesus in Luke 4:18, *"The Spirit of the Lord is upon me, because he hath anointed me to preach the gospel to the poor; he hath sent me to heal the brokenhearted, to preach deliverance to the captives, and recovering of sight to the blind, to set at liberty them that are bruised, to preach the acceptable year of the Lord."*

Jesus is our healing balm, the healer of our wounds. The heart of God our Father is to see us continually be made into His image and likeness, the likeness of

195

Jesus Christ. Jesus became an offering to the Father for our wounds and by His wounds we are healed. We should be a living sacrifice of praise to the Father and not a sacrifice to the wounds of our soul.

In Isaiah 1:5-6, the moral and spiritual condition of Israel was transferred to the suffering servant. Isaiah 53:4-5 says, *"Surely he hath borne our griefs, and carried our sorrows: yet we did esteem him stricken, smitten of God, and afflicted. 5 But he was wounded for our transgressions, he was bruised for our iniquities: the chastisement of our peace was upon him;* **and with his stripes we are healed.***"*

SET ASIDE TIME TO PRAY AND LISTEN

It is important to set aside time with God and tell Him about the pain of your wounds. In Matthew 7:7-8 Jesus invites us to ask God for anything.

"Ask, and it shall be given you, seek and ye shall find, knock and it shall be opened unto you: for everyone that asketh receiveth and he that seeketh findeth and to him that knocketh it shall be opened."

As you talk to the Lord about your wounds, ask Him to heal you and you shall receive your healing!

"Heavenly Father, please place your hand on my wounds and heal me, in Jesus name. May your Holy Spirit bring comfort to the deepest parts of me." In Jesus name, Amen!!!

Now, sit for a moment and listen to God's still small voice. What is the Lord speaking to you? Is there a scripture, song or memory that comes to mind?

_____

_____

_____

_____

_____

_____

_____

Therefore, I say to all,

➢ Be healed.

➢ Be made whole from the wounded spirit by the power of the blood of Jesus Christ.

➢ Receive, walk and live in your healing.

Now that you have received healing, know that you may be wounded again. But remember to continue to walk in a lifestyle of forgiveness and ask Jesus to heal your wound as soon as it occurs. The life you live is determined by the decisions you make in life, with or without Jesus Christ as your guide.

CHAPTER TWELVE
"Biblical Reconciliation & Restitution"

We must be healed and whole so that we are able to reproduce healed and whole disciples of the Gospel of Jesus Christ. How can you take anyone any further in the Lord than you are in Him? The Father's heart is for us to live a complete life in His love through Jesus Christ.

Paul writes in 2 Corinthians 5:18-19, *"And all things are of God, who hath **reconciled us to himself** by Jesus Christ, and hath given to us the **ministry of reconciliation**; 19 To wit, that God was in Christ, **reconciling the world unto himself**, not imputing their trespasses unto them; and hath committed unto us **the word of reconciliation**."*

When I think about reconciliation it brings me back to Genesis, *"In the beginning."* The depth of God's love was displayed when He stepped out of His Holy Temple to bring us back to Himself as He had promised when man fell in the garden. *Oh the garden scene*, when He made that promise in Genesis 3:15, *"And I will put enmity between thee and the woman, and between thy seed and her seed; **it shall bruise thy head**, and thou shalt bruise his heel."*

Jesus wants us to be so one with Him and the Father that He has imparted reconciliation in us, so that we can demonstrate it to others. This is why I **value forgiveness**, because I experienced God's love for me, first hand, when He allowed my children to confront and invite me to transform from that wounded unforgiving person. He saw me in a dead state. I was the walking dead, partying and living in the world, while thinking I was alright; yet He knew there was hope.

The ministry of reconciliation is evidence of God's wondrous love. It's an experience that once again brings me back to Genesis, when He spoke, *"Let there be **light**"*. He knew we were unable to keep the commandments given to Moses, so I AM came as Jesus. God's Word is life and became Flesh. John 1:1-5 announces, *"In the beginning was the Word, and the Word was with God, and the Word was God. 2 The same was in the beginning with God. 3 All things were made by him; and without him was not anything made that was made. 4 In him was life; and the life was the **light of men**. 5 And the **light shineth** in darkness; and the darkness comprehended it not."* This is the gospel. Are we willing to spread this gospel to the nations, as ministers of reconciliation?

I am confident that God has commissioned me, and I am committed to Him. Since I've acknowledged my sin, I am at liberty to share the gospel and present to you the need to be reconciled to God and others. I have overcome anger, bitterness, judging others, unforgiveness and so much more, by the blood of the Lamb and the word of my testimony (Revelation 12:11). As Psalm 119:11 says, *"Thy word have I hid in mine heart, that I might not sin against thee."*

Reconciliation happens between us and God when we receive Christ as our Savior. Reconciliation occurs with others when mutual respect and relationship is restored between individuals.

Is there anyone that you need to reconcile with?

_____

_____

_____

_____

_____

_____

_____

_____

_____

_____

_____

_____

_____

_____

RESTITUTION

Restitution is a fruit of repentance, where one chooses to make right a wrong committed against another. It is possible to have restitution without reconciliation. For example, in the case where a close friend steals jewelry from you. An act of restitution would be your friend returning the stolen jewelry. At that moment you may decide whether you want the relationship to be reconciled.

One day, while styling hair in my beauty parlor, I shared with a women about the troubles my ex-husband and I were having. I knew the story had gotten back to him and it had been exaggerated. It was very uncomfortable at first for me to ask him for his forgiveness, but God made it possible. The next step was for me to go back to her and clear his name. This was an act of restitution. Though our marriage was not reconciled, I chose to undo the damage I had imposed. It was a heart issue for me and by God's grace I did my part and was set free. Restitution may come with a physical offering or a peace offering.

Examples of Restitution:
➤ The person who murdered my loved one not only apologizes and repents but goes a step further to turn themselves into the police.
➤ Demonstration of being a changed person.
➤ You spoke lies and gossiped about a person or ministry publicly, so now you should publicly apologize and speak the truth, to clear their reputation.
➤ In a case of stealing, it is important to go back to the one it is stolen from in humility and

repentance and be willing to pay back or return the item stolen. Even if it is $5 a week to repay a greater debt, the person will know you truly want to repay your obligation.

It can be a difficult process, when making sure that your heart is right before men. If God reminds you of the people whom you may have hurt in past or present relationships, it is important that you do your best to 'make things right' through repentance and restitution, like in the case of Zacchaeus, the Tax Collector, in Luke 19:1-8.

*"And Jesus entered and passed through Jericho. And, behold, there was a man named Zacchaeus, which was the chief among the publicans, and he was rich. And he sought to see Jesus who he was; and could not for the press, because he was little of stature. And he ran before, and climbed up into a sycomore tree to see him: for he was to pass that way. And when Jesus came to the place, he looked up, and saw him, and said unto him, Zacchaeus, make haste, and come down; for today I must abide at thy house. And he made haste, and came down, and received him joyfully. And when they saw it, they all murmured, saying, that he was gone to be guest with a man that is a sinner. And Zacchaeus stood, and said unto the Lord: Behold, Lord, **the half of my goods I give to the poor; and if I have taken anything from any man by false accusation, I restore him fourfold"**.* Without Jesus asking, Zacchaeus voluntarily offered to bring restitution. I believe he was familiar with the instructions of Leviticus 6:2-5.

" If a soul sin, and commit a trespass against the LORD, and lie unto his neighbor in that which was

202

*delivered him to keep, or in fellowship, or in a thing taken away by violence, or hath deceived his neighbor; Or have found that which was lost, and lieth concerning it, and sweareth falsely; in any of all these that a man doeth, sinning therein: Then it shall be, because he hath sinned, and is guilty, **that he shall restore** that which he took violently away, or the thing which he hath deceitfully gotten, or that which was delivered him to keep, or the lost thing which he found, Or all that about which he hath sworn falsely; **he shall even restore it** in the principal, and shall add the fifth part more thereto, and give it unto him to whom it appertaineth, in the day of his trespass offering".*

In the case of a past relationship, where the other party may have been wounded by your words or actions, it is appropriate to repent to the person, by conversation or letter. This can be extremely challenging if you have had multiple broken relationships and/or if the persons are no longer in your life. In these cases, simply pray, "Jesus, if you allow the person(s) back in my pathway I am totally willing and committed to repent and make amends for my sins towards them." Be sure that you mean that prayer, because God may orchestrate those kinds of situations in our lives to ensure we are obedient to Him and what we have committed to do.

Why is restitution so important?

Restitution is important because it frees your heart from holding anything hidden in the darkness and it expresses God's heart through your example. It also lets the enemy know that he has no power to hold you in any form of bondage from past "hidden sins".

Do not be surprised if the people you are apologizing to, do not accept your apology or are not in agreement with your desire to make your wrong become right or want anything to do with you. In these situations, the most important thing is to have an attitude of humility and move on knowing that you are free because you did what was right in the sight of God. Making things right needs to be a constant flow in our hearts because it keeps our spirits sensitive to the Holy Spirit. By blocking out His voice or His nudging in our hearts, we are also hindering God from being able to completely flow in and through our lives.

APPLYING RESTITUTION

Take a moment to ask God, 'Is there anyone from my past or currently in my life that I need to repent and make amends with? Write down the names of those He reminds you of and go and make it right with them. It will not be easy, but it is definitely worth it. Matthew 5:23-24 is clear that *'if you bring your gift to the altar, and there remember that your brother has something against you, leave your gift there before the altar, and go your way. First be reconciled to your brother, and then come and offer your gift.'*

_____

_____

_____

_____

_____

_____

_____

_____

A very helpful practice is to write a letter to the person, detailing the account of offense. This letter is not necessarily to be shared with the individual, it is for you to hash everything out and be able to clearly evaluate the entire situation.

CHAPTER THIRTEEN
"Love After Forgiveness"

Forgiveness is an act of love. It is giving something that another may not deserve, just how we did not deserve Jesus to die for our sins. God gave love, when He gave us Christ (John 3:16). I have come to realize that in order to forgive others, it takes the type of love that only comes from God. Jesus taught us that as we ask God to forgive us, we must forgive those who trespass against us.

At the end of the Forgiveness Workshops that I host, I give every attendee a nail as a reminder of what Christ did for us on the cross. Saying, "He endured the pain of three nails on a cross for our sins."

The nail reminds us that we should love in action and in deed, through kindness. Be willing to give love at the risk of not receiving love. Also, don't allow pride to come in the way of you receiving the love that others want to pour into your life.

It's important to model love to the younger generation, through discipline, forgiveness, hospitality, kind speech, encouragement, teaching and other good works. I strive to continue living in love by demonstration to my children, grandchildren and others.

I believe that the portion of God's image that we were all made from is LOVE. This has helped me to share love on a wider scale than I was taught as a child. This love that God talks about is the greatest virtue any of us as believers could desire.

Love transcends language. Without saying a word, others will feel God's love through your presence. At this point in my life I want to clothe myself in God's love. I encourage you to evoke a life of love. 1 John 4:7-8 shows us that, *"Beloved, let us love one another: for love is of God; and every one that loveth is born of God, and knoweth God. He that loveth not knoweth not God; for **God is love**."*

Do not live a life fearful of loving and trusting again, because fear can keep you bound to your wounds. 2 Timothy 1:7 says, *"For God hath not given us the spirit of fear; but of power, and of love, and of a sound mind."* Jesus lived a life of love.

LOVE

God's love is shed abroad in our hearts. (Rom. 5:5)

God's love brings correction. (Hebrews 12:6-7)

Love covers a multitude of sins. (1 Peter 4:8)

Love does not harm. (Romans 13:10)

Love the Lord with your whole being. (Deut. 6:5)

Love your neighbor. (Leviticus 19:18)

Love righteousness. (Psalm 45:7)

Love bears all things. (1 Corinthians 13:7)

Love believes all things. (1 Corinthians 13:7)

Love hopes in all things. (1 Corinthians 13:7)

Love endures all things. (1 Corinthians 13:7)

Love suffers long. (1 Corinthians 13:4)

Love is kind. (1 Corinthians 13:4)

Love does not envy. (1 Corinthians 13:4)

Love never fails. (1 Corinthians 13:8)

Love is not prideful. (1Corinthians 13:4)

"Not as though I had already attained, either were already perfect: but I follow after, if that I may apprehend that for which also, I am apprehended of Christ Jesus. Brethren, I count not myself to have apprehended: but this one thing I do, forgetting those things which are behind, and reaching forth unto those things which are before, I press toward the mark for the prize of the high calling of God in Christ Jesus. Let us therefore, as many as be perfect, be thus minded: and if in anything ye be otherwise minded, God shall reveal even this unto you. Nevertheless, whereto we have already attained, let us walk by the same rule, let us mind the same thing". Philippians 3:12-16

TOOLKIT FOR STAYING FREE

PRAYER OF DELIVERANCE

I cover myself with the blood of Jesus and put on the whole armor of God, protecting my mind with the helmet of salvation. I put on the belt of truth, the shield of faith, the sword of the spirit, which is Your Word, the breastplate of righteousness and I put on the shoes of peace that comes from the Good News. I come against every fiery dart of the enemy by the power of the blood of Jesus'.

Lord, I take authority over my thoughts, and command that they will line up with God's truth over my life. I stand against the patterns of fear, doubt, and unbelief and command them to flee from my life now in Jesus' name. I declare that I am a man/ woman of faith, confident hope and belief in your word.

I command all roots of unforgiveness, anger and bitterness to leave me right now. I command all mental, emotional and physical wounds, torments, and trauma to flee from my life now in Jesus' name. I renounce all ancestral sins in my life and break off its power over my life. I commit to being a new creation in Christ and declare that I will not live in the sins of my parents or generations prior.

I thank you Lord, that Your promise to me is that goodness and mercy shall follow me all the days of my life and that no weapon that is formed against me will prosper because You have already paid the ultimate price for my sins.

Thank you Lord, for this new life of freedom, in Jesus' name. Amen.

"O LORD my God, I cried unto thee, and thou hast healed me. O LORD, thou hast brought up my soul from the grave: thou hast kept me alive, that I should not go down to the pit". (Psalm 30:2-3).

SPIRITUAL SURGERY PRAYER

The Lord walked me through Spiritual Surgery using Psalm 27, Psalm 51 and Psalm 91.

Psalm 27

I DECLARE THAT the LORD is my light and my salvation; whom shall I fear? the LORD is the strength of my life; of whom shall I be afraid? 4 One thing have I desired of the LORD, that will I seek after; that I may dwell in the house of the LORD all the days of my life, to behold the beauty of the LORD, and to enquire in his temple. 6 And now shall mine head be lifted up above mine enemies round about me: therefore will I offer in his tabernacle sacrifices of joy; I will sing, yea, I will sing praises unto the LORD. 7 Hear, O LORD, when I cry with my voice: have mercy also upon me, and answer me. 8 When thou saidst, Seek ye my face; my heart said unto thee, Thy face, LORD, will I seek. 10 When my father and my mother forsake me, then the LORD will take me up. 13 I had fainted, unless I had believed to see the goodness of the LORD in the land of the living. 14 Wait on the LORD: be of good courage, and he shall strengthen thine heart: wait, I say, on the LORD.

Psalm 51

Have mercy upon me, O God, according to thy lovingkindness: according unto the multitude of thy tender mercies blot out my transgressions. 2 Wash me thoroughly from mine iniquity, and cleanse me from my sin. 3 For I acknowledge my transgressions: and my sin is ever before me. 4 Against thee, thee only, have I sinned, and done this evil in thy sight:

that thou mightest be justified when thou speakest, and be clear when thou judgest. 7 Purge me with hyssop, and I shall be clean: wash me, and I shall be whiter than snow. 10 Create in me a clean heart, O God; and renew a right spirit within me. 13 Then will I teach transgressors thy ways; and sinners shall be converted unto thee. 14 Deliver me from bloodguiltiness, O God, thou God of my salvation: and my tongue shall sing aloud of thy righteousness. 17 The sacrifices of God are a broken spirit: a broken and a contrite heart, O God, thou wilt not despite

Psalm 91

He that dwelleth in the secret place of the most High shall abide under the shadow of the Almighty. 2 I will say of the LORD, He is my refuge and my fortress: my God; in him will I trust. 3 Surely he shall deliver thee from the snare of the fowler, and from the noisome pestilence. 4 He shall cover thee with his feathers, and under his wings shalt thou trust: his truth shall be thy shield and buckler. 7 A thousand shall fall at thy side, and ten thousand at thy right hand; but it shall not come nigh thee. 9 Because thou hast made the LORD, which is my refuge, even the most High, thy habitation; 10 There shall no evil befall thee, neither shall any plague come nigh thy dwelling. 11 For he shall give his angels charge over thee, to keep thee in all thy ways. 14 Because he hath set his love upon me, therefore will I deliver him: I will set him on high, because he hath known my name. 15 He shall call upon me, and I will answer him: I will be with him in trouble; I will deliver him, and honour him. 16 With long life will I satisfy him, and shew him my salvation.

IN JESUS NAME I PRAY, AMEN.

PRAYER OF COMFORT

Psalm 23

The LORD is my shepherd; I shall not want. He maketh me to lie down in green pastures; He leadeth me beside the still waters. He restoreth my soul: He leadeth me in the paths of righteousness for His name's sake. Yea, though I walk through the valley of the shadow of death, I will fear no evil: for thou art with me; thy rod and thy staff, they comfort me. Thou preparest a table before me in the presence of mine enemies: thou anointest my head with oil; my cup runneth over. Surely goodness and mercy shall follow me all the days of my life: and I will dwell in the house of the LORD, forever,

DECLARATION

I declare that from this day forward I will walk in God's complete desire and will for my life which is to live and walk fully free in Him.

I declare and decree that who the Son sets free is free indeed. I am the head and not the tail, above and not beneath. I am a royal priesthood, a peculiar person and a chosen generation to declare the praises of God. I am fearfully and wonderfully made.

I declare and decree that God's plans for my life are to prosper and not to harm me. No weapon formed against me shall prosper and every tongue that rises up against me shall be condemned. I am a new creation in Christ. Thank you that Your Word says that ***"you will restore to me the years that the locust has eaten, the cankerworms and the caterpillars and palmerworms". (Joel 2:25)***.

I thank you Lord that from this day forward, surely goodness and mercy shall follow me all the days of my life, as I dwell in the house of the Lord forever. Behold, old things have passed away and now I am made new because of Christ's love and forgiveness in my life. Thank you, Jesus, for this new life of freedom. In Jesus name I pray, Amen.

ALABASTER OIL

"And being in Bethany in the house of Simon the leper, as he sat at meat, there came a woman having an alabaster box of ointment of spikenard very precious; and she broke the box, and poured it on his head. And there were some that had indignation within themselves, and said, why was this waste of the ointment made? For it might have been sold for more than three hundred pence, and have been given to the poor. And they murmured against her. And Jesus said," let her alone; why trouble ye her? She hath wrought a good work on me". Mark 14:3-6.

"And one of the Pharisees desired him that he would eat with him. And he went into the Pharisee's house, and sat down to meat. And, behold, a woman in the city, which was a sinner, when she knew that Jesus sat at meat in the Pharisee's house, brought an alabaster box of ointment. Luke 7:36-37

As I planned my 50th Birthday Party, I listened to a song that spoke about the cost of the oil in the Alabaster Box. I reminisced about all the Lord had done for me and likened myself unto Mary Magdalena, who took spikenard oil valued at a year's wages and poured it on Jesus' head. I invite you to use this story in the Bible as a guide to creating your own alabaster box.

Place in the box: CDs, DVDs, journals, and words of prophecy, testimonies, and anything else the Lord has used to minister to you personally. I have accumulated things that have happened in my life, such as Holy Spirit giving me a song, scripture, or prophetic word.

All of these bring me to Revelation 12:11, **"and they overcame him by the blood of the Lamb and _by the word of their testimony_;..."** I have overcome some stuff and that is my testimony! When difficult and hurtful things were happening, I didn't know it was working together for my good as a part of my calling by God (Romans 8:28).

CONSECRATION PRAYER

Lord Jesus, I come as your daughter/son, seeking to draw closer to You in my heart. Therefore, Lord, I am asking for Your Holy Spirit to bring conviction to my heart and reveal any area which needs cleansing. Blessed Holy Spirit, I repent for not always being open to Your Holy Spirit's nudging and leading in my life and for listening to the voice of the enemy. I want to respond only to the sound of your still small voice as you alert me. I am determined to no longer be a tool for the enemy to use, but will be a channel for the Holy Spirit to flow in and through.

Wash me clean from my guilt, and purify me from my sins. Create in me a clean heart, O God; and renew a right spirit within me. I am a warrior for the Kingdom of God and will remain faithful and obedient to do all that you ask of me. Empower me O Lord, to be all that I can be through the Blood of Jesus. I will position myself as a woman/man of God, so that I can distinguish the "noise" of distraction from Your voice. Anoint me with integrity, wisdom, knowledge, love and joy needed to fulfill my destiny. Help me to see that you have already impregnated me with a vision and a calling to please you, Lord. Help me to walk in the fullness of Your plan for my life; having an unoffendable heart; and I am asking you for the joy of the Lord to be my strength as I continue in faith living by the power of the blood of Jesus Christ.

In Your Mighty name, Jesus! Amen and Amen!

Take a moment and think about your life and your future. Is there anything else you want to say to the Lord or repent of as you are asking God to consecrate you?

_____

_____

_____

_____

_____

_____

_____

_____

_____

_____

_____

_____

_____

DAILY PRAYER

Prayer taken from <u>Developing the Fruit of Patience Longsuffering, 30 Day Devotional</u>.

Heavenly Father, You are holy, I glorify You in the beauty of Your Holiness. Thank you for loving, protecting, caring and providing for my family and me. When times are good, I will praise you! When times are difficult, I will praise you! I will honor and exalt You in every circumstance.
Let your kingdom come and will be done in my life, as it is in Heaven. Cause your purpose to be fulfilled in me. I choose to seek you first and invite Precious Holy Spirit to develop His fruit in my life.
Continue to provide for my family, friends, neighbors, and myself all that we need today. May there be more than enough to share with others.
Search my heart, and show me what hidden sin is in my life. As I confess each one to you, purify me in Your presence and create in me a clean heart and renew a right spirit within me.
I forgive my enemies and friends who have hurt, angered, offended or betrayed me and ask that you would have mercy on them and bless them.
Please forgive me of all my evil thoughts, words and actions. I recognize that my sin hurts, angers, offends and betrays You.
Teach me your ways, that I might not sin against You. Inscribe Your word on my heart and mind, that all of my ways, would be pleasing to you.
Do not lead me into temptation, but deliver me from all evil.
To you, Oh Mighty Yahweh, belongs the kingdom, the power and the glory, in Yahshua's name.

Go to WWW.SUZANNEMARCELLUS.COM to find books in the Developing the Fruit of the Spirit, A Journey Through the Heart of Christ series, written by Suzanne Phillippa Marcellus.

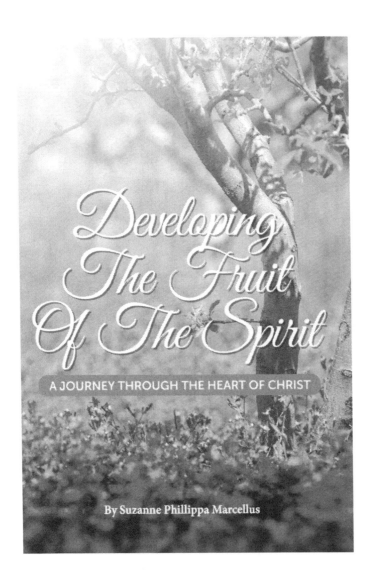

ADDITIONAL NOTES:

_____

_____

_____

_____

_____

_____

_____

_____

_____

_____

_____

_____

_____

_____

_____

"Lift up your heads, O ye gates; and be ye lift up, ye everlasting doors; and the King of glory shall come in. ⁸ Who is this King of glory? The LORD strong and mighty, the LORD mighty in battle. ⁹ Lift up your heads, O ye gates; even lift them up, ye everlasting doors; and the King of glory shall come in. ¹⁰ Who is this King of glory? The LORD of hosts, he is the King of glory. Selah."

Psalm 24:7-10

ABOUT THE AUTHOR

Winsome Leona Williams, also known as 'Mama Cheery" was born in St. Andrew, Jamaica W.I. on December 18, 1954 to parents, Winston and Elaine Mullings, thus given the name Winsome from her father's name. The word 'winsome' means charming. God has graced her with a dynamic personality which she has used to reach out in evangelism, missionary work and hospitality. Leona is derived from the word 'lionesses. There is no doubt that God has blessed her with His super-natural strength so that she can be a blessing to others especially in the area of intercession. It has been prophesied and declared over her life that she carries a 'Deborah spirit'.

In order to be an effective leader, there are four basic qualities we must have and like Deborah, Winsome possesses these qualities:

Obedient to the voice of God: After being a licensed cosmetologist for 30 years, God called Winsome to full-time ministry. She then released her profitable business, which she owned for over 10 years. The Bible says *'in all your ways acknowledge him and he shall direct your paths'* (Proverbs 3:6). For Winsome, being obedient to the Holy Spirit is non-negotiable.

Initiative to implement: When Winsome's daughter, Tanique told her about the forgiveness training she attended during her discipleship training, the Holy Spirit led her to share with her mother because she knew her mother was carrying around unforgiveness towards her (Tanique's) father. God broke down the walls of unforgiveness in Winsome's life through repentance and restitution and later called her to teach on forgiveness. After receiving her training through the Holy Spirit, she took the initiative and launched her ministry 'In His Will Ministries of South Florida'. She has ministered in Haiti, Santo Domingo, Jamaica, Israel, regions in South East Asia and various states within USA

Supportive of leadership: Winsome was appointed as the Youth Pastor of Open Bible Community Church (OBCC) in 2004. Today, she remains a Pastoral Ministry Team member at the church and carries more of a supportive role in the lives of youth while walking out God's call on her life. In her workshops, she joins forces with other leaders so that together they can reach a broader audience. Her objectives are to reach people for the Lord and to see lives changed through forgiveness and restoration.

Faith to trust God: Every day for her is a 'faith walk'. She does not give thought of what she will eat or what she will drink, because she knows that God will meet her needs according to His riches in Glory, therefore she gives and expects nothing in return. When you grace her house with your presence, you can feel the love of God "bursting through its walls". A Culinary artist by nature, she feeds her guests with food that is 'fit for a king' as she is inspired by the Holy Spirit. There is no lack in her life, spiritually or physically because she trusts the Lord with all her heart. She is a 'Ruth' to many of her sisters and a 'Naomi' to others, but to all of God's people she is a mighty woman of God who is charged by Jesus and is committed to serve.

Nina Hart,
Author/Speaker

Printed in Great Britain
by Amazon